# IN LOVE

CULTIVATING QUALITIES FOR A LOVE THAT LASTS A LIFETIME

BUD CALVERT

All Scripture quotations are taken from the King James Version. Special emphasis in verses is added.



The author and publication team have put forth every effort to give proper credit to quotes and thoughts that are not original with the author. It is not our intent to claim originality with any quote or thought that could not readily be tied to an original source.

First edition printing 2016 in the United States

Cover design and typesetting by Jenneth Dyck

ISBN 979-8-218-26625-7

Printed in the United States of America

# DEDICATION

Heart-felt gratitude and love go to my wife, Mary. Without her love, encouragement, and support, this book would not have been a possibility. We are now past the heavenly milestone of fifty years of marriage, by seven years, and although we don't claim to have "arrived," Mary and I are still praising the Lord for all He has done! We continue to serve our Lord, together, through our local church here in Southwest Florida. "Whoso findeth a wife findeth a good thing, and obtaineth favour of the Lord" (Proverbs 18:22).

# CONTENTS

## ACKNOWLEDGMENTS

My sincere thanks to Pastor Kyle Fannin and Bluegrass Baptist Church, which he founded in 2008, for his encouragement in having this book reformatted, edited and published. He and his wife, Jessica, are prime examples of a godly couple serving each other, their family, and their church in Georgetown, Kentucky. I am also grateful for Jenneth Dyck and her know-how in formatting and designing the book.

# PREFACE

Marriages—Christian marriages—are breaking up at alarming rates. Today, rather than celebrating twenty-five or fifty years as milestone anniversaries, we are now honoring those who have survived for five or ten years. Anniversaries have become a recognition of survival, rather than a celebration of lifetime love.

My primary purpose in writing these pages is to give hope and encouragement to every Christian marriage. The hope for our homes is in Jesus Christ alone, whom the Bible calls our "blessed hope" (Titus 2:13). The fact that our hope is alive is indeed encouraging. First Peter 1:3 teaches that when the Lord saved our souls, He brought us "unto a lively [living] hope by the resurrection of Jesus Christ from the dead." The resurrected Jesus is our *living hope.*

Thus, I want to share biblical principles that offer assurance to every couple that—regardless of the difficulty, struggle, or even atrocious offenses in their home—there is hope! You really can experience a lifetime of being "in love."

The second purpose of this book is to provide a picture for how godly couples can enjoy life and one another. Second Peter 1:3 again instructs us that God has "given unto us all things that pertain unto life and godliness, through the knowledge of him that hath called us to glory and virtue." Everything we will ever need to know about life and joyful Christian living can be found in God's Word (although I would like for you to continue reading this book!).

The Bible is our final authority. Knowing that the precepts for successful family living are found in Scripture, we have only to look to God for our solutions. He has given us everything we need to resolve problems and live victoriously through His Word.

This book will address many practical applications from God's Word to Christian marriages. In this way, it will be more of a "hands-on" help than a philosophical treatise. The principles providing the bedrock for each chapter are derived directly from the Word of God and are intended to aid the couple who have put their faith in Jesus Christ as Saviour and is seeking to follow Him.

If you have not yet made the heart decision to believe in Jesus Christ, you will read in the following pages what it means to have a relationship with Him. And, I hope you will make the choice to do so, for without a personal relationship with the Author of the Bible, you will never be able to do what He says and requires for a happy, joy-filled marriage.

No matter where you are on your spiritual or marital

journey, I would encourage you to approach this book with a spirit of discovery and intent. God's Word has the answers, and I am honored to share them with you. It is my prayer that you will be helped, as I have, as you read this book, not because of *my* writings, but because of *His*.

# PART 1

# THE SUPREME NEED

## The Systematic Practice of Biblical Communication

# In Love

Apart from a saving knowledge of Jesus Christ, what *is* the supreme need of every family? While some husbands may assert, "It's to get my wife to follow my leadership," countless wives are thinking, "My greatest need is to have a husband who loves me unconditionally." Others may point to more money, a bigger home, a better job, more disciplined children, and the list could go on. All people have some idea as to what will make them truly happy in their marriage and home.

Many years in the ministry, counseling families undergoing stressful situations of all kinds, have proven to me that the supreme need of every home is *the systematic practice of biblical communication*. Most husbands and wives simply do not take the time to share their thoughts and feelings within a biblical context—in fact, many do not share them in *any* context. Yet, biblical communication knits the thoughts, desires, wills, and emotions of two individuals into one integrated whole. Sound communication produces love in the home.

Parenthetically, biblical communication also produces oneness in a church. Church unity stems from the oneness enjoyed in the individual homes of the church family. How many problems could be resolved within a church family if members sought a resolution to their problems biblically, rather than emotionally or even rationally? We are far too prone to resort to our own ways of doing things, based on *our* thoughts and *our* feelings and *our* rationale. Isaiah 55:8–9 reveals how small our ways are in contrast to God's: "For my thoughts are not your thoughts, neither are your ways my ways, saith the LORD. For as the heavens are higher than the earth, so are my ways higher than your ways, and my thoughts than your thoughts." The key, then, is for us to search the Bible to find God's thoughts and God's ways so that we can think and live them in our marriages and homes.

## WE HAVE PROBLEMS

Several factors regularly contribute to the communication breakdown most families experience. Scheduling conflicts with children's sports and music requirements, work with all of its nuances, paying bills, and the general busyness and requirements of life, all pull us away from real, heartfelt communication.

Perhaps the chief culprit today is the electronic world, whether it be the tv, computer, smart phone, tablet, or the various other electronic gadgets and games that young and old alike allow to occupy their time and lives. Many have immersed themselves into social media without developing the communication skills that result from engaging in direct face-to-face dialog.

The family has never been as disjointed as it is today. A husband may wake at 5:30 AM, leave for work at 6:30 AM, and be gone for eleven or more hours. He comes home to his wife, who often just got home and started preparing supper in the kitchen, with one child practicing the trombone (which is driving Dad crazy), one child on the Internet, another child off at soccer practice, and the other one somewhere off in the neighborhood playing with friends. At this point, it is virtually impossible to get everyone around the table to enjoy a family dinner.

And then there are the families where one or more of them insists on having dinner in front of the television or answering a text on the phone, which stays in their lap during supper. Is it any wonder these people have a family communication problem?

The communication problems are compounded if, once dinner is over, the family members go their separate ways to do homework, clean up the kitchen, read the paper, or prop themselves in front of the television or computer, often absorbing the trash and ungodly philosophies the devil purveys through these mediums. If a family is having any kind of communication problem, one of the first practical places to look to change is the electronic world. Similarly, newspapers and periodicals, while not necessarily bad, can be harmful if read during meals and allowed to encroach upon other family time.

If both husband and wife work, the strain that work entails may yield additional communication difficulties.

I read about one couple that was having major problems getting along, so the woman had enough and finally went to talk to her pastor to let him know that as far as she was concerned, their marriage was over. Since they were new to the church and the pastor didn't know their situation, he inquired if she had grounds. She said, "Yes. We have about an acre and a half."

The pastor then said, "That's not what I'm after. What I mean is do you have some kind of a grudge with him?"

She responded, "No, but we do have a carport."

Thinking there might be some kind of abuse going on, the pastor said, "Sister, that's not what I'm asking. Does he beat you up?"

"No. I get up before him every morning!"

Then in exasperation he said, "Lady, what I'm asking is what is the problem in your marriage?"

She finally said, "We can't seem to communicate with each other!"

Poor communication can indeed become a source of major frustration. Each family should examine its own routine to discover the origin of its communication problem. Living in the information technology age presents a whole new set of challenges added to the age-old struggles involving money, drugs, abuse, culture, sex, relationships, rebellion, anger, bitterness, loneliness, heartaches, divorce, and death.

## THERE IS HOPE

Pastoring in the Washington, D.C. area at the seat of our nation's government and military is different because most people only live there three or four years before they move on. Because of the transitory nature of the area, many people are only there for a short time, but long enough for many marriages to experience the strain of pressure, politics, and power. When exasperation set in couples would come in for counseling, and sometimes the husband would sit at one end of the couch and the wife at the other. Their countenances would be stern and their bodies rigid as they announced, "Pastor, our marriage is hopeless. There is no way we can resolve our differences." Some had already consulted divorce attorneys. Others were separated and wanted confirmation that their marriage was a predicament beyond resolution.

I don't believe that a marriage where both people are Christians can ever be lost beyond hope. In fact, have you ever stopped to analyze the difference between a Christian home and one where Christ is not preeminent? The biggest difference between a saved and an unsaved couple is that the saved couple has Jesus Christ and His Word. We have the Holy Spirit who is able and willing, yea wanting, to work in our families and individual lives. Therefore, whatever the nature of a couple's problem, with God's help, it can be resolved through effectual, biblical communication. There *is* hope!

Succinctly put, communication is the process of sharing verbally *and* nonverbally one's thoughts and experiences. It is the sharing and exchanging of information with others. And since this section addresses the supreme need of *biblical* communication, we will be talking about communicating in such a manner that we don't violate Scripture or biblical principles.

Communication involves becoming a part of another person's life. The more conscious we become of another person's needs, the more we can love, pray, and care for that person. It involves more than talking—it also means listening.

ONE

# A Fresh Start

So, how *can* we better establish good, biblical communication in the home in order to achieve love that lasts for a lifetime? How can we *stay* in love throughout a multi-decade, lifelong marriage? The following suggestions, when followed, will better equip the Christian couple and family to accomplish this goal. Moreover, they will aid the family in fulfilling its responsibilities before God.

## COMMITMENT

Commitment to communicate is an absolute must for all couples who intend to stay in love. Don't think that because you have—and express—differences from time to time, your marriage or family is "really bad." Having been a member of the human race for over seventy years, I can tell you that every couple and family have had or will have struggles and difficulties to work through. The only difference between the relationship that my wife and I enjoy as I write this and those who struggle due to personal differences is that Mary and I have no unresolved conflicts of any kind between us. It doesn't mean we haven't had conflicts or that we won't have any in the future; it simply means that we have learned and applied the principles in the Bible to resolve any problems that may arise. Chapters 2–8 of this book delineate twenty-one biblical principles that will foster good communication. Review these principles as husband and wife, and make a commitment to God and to one another to employ them when communicating. In fact, now would be a good time to put this book down, get on your knees and commit to the Lord that you are going to learn and apply His communication principles in your marriage.

## THE COMMUNICATION SESSION

Have you ever felt completely in the dark regarding a marital problem, either because you couldn't fully articulate your own issues or didn't understand those of your spouse? We've all been there. Often it is simply easier to remain in a state of denial than to face the facts. So, the first big step for a couple to take is to admit there are problems between them. One spouse can be a complete optimist, thinking everything is just wonderful, while the other is crying and screaming inside because of the unresolved offenses. Or, it may be that both spouses readily admit that something is wrong. In any case, this first step of acknowledging your marital problems is essential for you to get your relationship back on track.

The question is often posed, "But, we've already tried communicating, with no result. Why try again?" The answer is that *this* time, contrary to any previous attempt, the dialogue will be grounded in biblical truth. We're not just talking about magic phrases to use to get your spouse's attention or tricks to make your spouse see the situation from your angle. Unfortunately, many adults have not had parents or other influential couples who modeled good communication. As a result, we've seen failed attempts of resolution time and time again and think failure is unavoidable. But, if the dialogue falters, it is because someone ignored a biblical truth (which we will discuss in Part 2). Biblical communication is *learned* behavior—it doesn't come to us just because we are Christians.

A good exercise here for all couples—and usually one of the first assignments I give when counseling couples—is for each spouse to write down what he/she considers to be ten (or one, or twenty-five, or any number of) unresolved problems. This list can then be used when the two of you sit down to tenderly discuss issues, as we will address in the coming chapters.

So, how do we begin? This will likely seem somewhat formal, but every couple should try to find a place and time to meet together for the purpose of discussing and resolving problems. It would probably be best at first not to meet in a public place such as a restaurant, since the problems discussed may be emotionally charged. Choose any place in the house where you can have quality discussion time—without the children, phone, or television competing for attention. A table to write on would be helpful.

The goal here is not to add rigidity, but discipline and structure. For this reason, be sure to make the time and place a mutually agreed-upon decision. It makes no difference whether you have been married six months or sixty years—if you have unresolved problems of any kind with your spouse, this exercise will help you.

## THE SESSION AGENDA

Each time you sit down for the purpose of communicating and solving a problem(s), you should start with a word of prayer. This should be followed by the reading of Ephesians 4:22–32 and a review of the principles contained therein (more on this in the next chapter). It would help to read this passage daily, seeking to learn new precepts from God's Word while reviewing those already studied. Performing these preliminary actions helps create the proper atmosphere for problem-solving together.

Always begin your communication session with low-stress discussions: a list of the day's events, phone calls, or personal mail received, people met, amusing incidents with the children, and so on. An excellent topic might also be a special blessing or insight culled from one's personal devotions that day. Again, while these preliminary tips may seem obvious to read and awkward to implement, they are important steps to take before leaping into the list of unresolved conflicts.

Next on the agenda, then, is a list of unresolved conflicts. Both individuals need to be honest at this point. If a marital relationship has drifted for years without the anchor of biblical communication, many outstanding problems have likely been suppressed in bitterness or animosity. These must be dealt with. The Bible says "love covereth all sins" (Proverbs 10:12b). If old scores still needle one score or the other, then love has yet to cover these sins. This is not to suggest that you should rummage through your old "problem closet" to emerge with ten-year-old grievances. It does mean, however, that any offense weakening the bond between the two individuals should be noted on their combined agenda and should be biblically settled at this or a future communication time. Ephesians 4:29 says, "Let no corrupt communication proceed out of your mouth, but that which is good to the use of edifying, that it may minister grace unto the hearers." Some offenses, because of their very nature, should not be aired, but should rather be confessed privately to God. (This will be discussed briefly in chapter 6.)

The next step is to decide which problems will be tackled first. At the initial session, each individual may have a list of ten to twenty problems he or she would like to discuss. Together the couple should peruse these topics, organize them according to their importance, and begin discussing them one by one. I would suggest that each person pick out the top one or two things he or she wants to deal with first. Remember, a communication time is for the sole purpose of *resolving* problems, not *creating* them. It is not a time for loudly proving one's point, but instead is a time for demonstrating respect and love for your spouse. Do not win the battle only to lose the war.

If an issue proves thorny, requiring more than one session to settle, simply decide to table it and continue it the next time.

Problems that have festered for years are seldom resolved in one half-hour interval. Recognize this need and, without stockpiling the problem (which God expressly condemns in Ephesians 4:26), carry it over to the following night's agenda.

You might be thinking right about now, "This seems to be awfully mechanical—where's the heart?" As in any situation, when we are dealing with emotions, rationales, problems, and feelings, there will be some tense moments. But once the basics are experienced and put into practice, it will become much more natural, and you will be able to establish your own format. Be patient and give yourself and your spouse time.

This "conference table" is a place to confer, not to argue. Begin by talking about yourself, your sins and failures, and settle all such matters first by asking forgiveness where you know you have been wrong, even if you don't realize it until you see it through your spouse's eyes.

Ask also for help (Matthew 7:4–5). Direct all your energies toward defeating the problem, not toward the other person. Your goal is to reach biblical solutions, so always have Bibles on the table and use them. It helps to record the results of your work on paper.[1]

At the conclusion of your problem-solving time, always close with a prayer and a kiss! The kiss will be the barometer for gauging the session's success. If biblical communication has been achieved, a couple will gladly embrace. If the kiss is unwelcome, one of the twenty-one principles in the following chapters has been violated. This offense should then be identified and resolved so the couple can still end the session with a happy embrace.

# PART 2
# BIBLICAL CHANGE

Do not think you are alone if your marriage is not all it should be. The sad reality is that all marriages struggle and approximately one of two marriages now ends in divorce. This is not because today's dilemmas are new or because God is incapable of helping. Rather, the responsibility for this may lie in the average couple's complaints:

"We can't seem to communicate."

"We are not compatible."

"We are so different."

"We don't get along."

Part One of this book established a physical framework for resolving these complaints—the commitment, the communication session, and the agenda. Now we will explore the fundamentals of biblical communication itself.

## I DON'T FEEL LIKE IT

Frequently, when problems appear in the home, the individuals resort to their "old natures" to address the problems, operating from a feeling-oriented, rather than an action-oriented perspective. The problem with this method is that depending on feelings for direction will ultimately prove unsatisfactory, for there will be times when you simply don't feel like doing right, even though God has commanded it. While sulking and pity parties, for instance, may seem to help one spouse or the other to personally get through a given situation, these feeling-oriented behaviors ultimately solve nothing and weaken the relationship long term.

Contrary to what you may have heard or thought, acting biblically (in accordance with Scripture) is never sinful or hypocritical, even when your heart is not in it. There may be times you don't *feel* like reading your Bible, responding in love when someone verbally attacks you, or going to work, church, or school when you are supposed to. When you do the right thing, however, God is pleased, and you are obedient. In other words, doing right according to the Bible even when you don't *feel* like it is not living a lie—it is being obedient regardless of the circumstances. While obedience may *look* like hypocrisy sometimes, it never is when you are doing it with a desire to honor God regardless of your feelings. It is doing what you know is right, in accordance with the Scriptures, even though you may not *feel* like doing it. And, while having the right attitude *is* important, you may find yourself without the energy to muster a good attitude even while obeying. You are still obeying because it is right, and that is not hypocrisy.

Hypocrisy is when you pretend to be someone or something you are not. Prior to becoming a Christian I tried "turning over a new leaf" and living a better life. I did my best to "look" like a Christian, but I had no power to be one. I had several bad habits that I tried to stop but to no avail. When I first met Mary at a church, one dear lady told Mary that I was a "wonderful Christian young man." Although I appreciated her endorsement, I was just good at hypocrisy.

The basic error of feeling-oriented people is that they believe that the feelings themselves become the final authority and the motivation as to whether or not something gets done. So, it is of utmost importance as we seek to heal and/or strengthen our marriages, we choose to obey biblical principles and mandates, no matter how we feel.

## THE BEST INSURANCE FOR A LASTING MARRIAGE

The most important relationship anyone ever undertakes is the relationship formed with Jesus Christ, the Son of God. This relationship of becoming a child of God (John 1:12) begins with a decision, and it takes place the moment you decide to put your faith and trust in the Lord Jesus Christ for forgiveness of sins and eternity with Him in Heaven.

The "gospel" is simply believing that "Christ died for our sins according to the scriptures; And that he was buried, and that he arose again the third day according to the scriptures" (1 Corinthians 15:3–4). Our salvation is based strictly on the finished work of Jesus Christ, in His shed blood and resurrection for our sins to be forgiven. No matter how sincere or good someone is, without the saving grace of God, there is no hope. Paul, writing under the inspiration of God, said "For by grace are ye saved through faith; and that not of yourselves: it is the gift of God: Not of works, lest any man should boast" (Ephesians 2:8–9). Baptism, catechism, church membership, or clean, moral living will not—and cannot—help at all. Salvation is a gift of God; and a gift, by its very nature, cannot be bought or worked for. We sinned ("For all have sinned, and come short of the glory of God" Romans 3:23); there is a price on sin ("For the wages of sin is death" Romans 6:23a); Jesus paid that price ("But God commendeth his love toward us, in that, while we were yet sinners, Christ died for us" Romans 5:8); and we receive that gift through believing the gospel ("but the gift of God is eternal life through Jesus Christ our Lord" Romans 6:23b).

Salvation is a matter of the heart; it is a relationship—not a religion. After spending three years in the United States Army as a paratrooper, I returned home and started attending a church with my mom and siblings. It was there, at a weekend camp for singles, that I was confronted with this heart issue of having a relationship with Jesus Christ. Romans 10:10 says, "For with the heart man believeth unto righteousness...." I always had "head" knowledge (I believed the Bible and that Jesus was resurrected from the dead), but it never reached the heart to transform my life. In other words, I never acted upon that knowledge.

If you have not yet made the decision to trust Christ as your personal Saviour, I would encourage you to do that immediately. Without a saving relationship with Christ, you may implement some common sense truths that could even help your marriage, but you'll not have the dynamic grace of God enabling you to act on Bible principles.

Marriage, the second most important relationship of life, also begins with a decision—the decision of whom God would have you marry. Once the Lord has led in this decision and you marry, a covenant is made before God and before witnesses that the bond will be permanent. You may be thinking, "So, *that's* it. I didn't marry the one God would have chosen for me, so I need to dump my wife/husband now and get in line for God's choice!" Sorry, although you may have married outside the will of God or before you became a Christian, it is God's perfect will for you now to stay married.

"But how can I be certain my marriage will last?" one might ask. The answer is, that without help from God, you cannot be certain. It is nearly impossible unless the two individuals follow the principles of the Word of God for their lives. It is only then that we can make a positive judgment on an enduring relationship. Making a commitment to God to follow the precepts set forth in His Word is the best insurance for a lasting marriage. Keep in mind, Christians are divorcing at the same rate now as the unsaved which simply means we are failing God and His Word, not the other way around.

The last three chapters of Ephesians give us some intensely practical pointers on how to live the Christian life. Ephesians 4:22–32 delineates twenty-one principles that relate directly to biblical communication, as well as to the perfecting of our spiritual journey toward a lifelong loving marriage. If each member of your family will seek to apply these principles, which we will briefly examine one at a time, home life is guaranteed to improve.

And one more thing: right before the Bible sets forth the twenty-one principles, the Holy Spirit presents us with a critical axiom—"the truth is in Jesus" (Ephesians 4:21). We are absolutely assured that whatever principles are gleaned from God's Word are *truth,* providing life, hope, and direction for every situation.

TWO

# Off with the Old, On with the New

Echoing through the halls of discontent is an oft-heard argument: "I've got my rights. If I don't stand up for myself, who will?" The truth is, a growing Christian is willing to surrender his *rights* and assume *responsibilities* in his relationships. One of our first responsibilities in marriage is to abandon the old, selfish way of living and to begin preferring one another. Romans 12:10 says, "Be kindly affectioned one to another with brotherly love; in honor preferring one another." And Ephesians 4 gives us several very specific ways to do this. Let's take a look at the principles found in Ephesians 4.

## PRINCIPLE 1: PUT OFF THE OLD MAN

"That ye put off concerning the former conversation the old man, which is corrupt according to the deceitful lusts" (Ephesians 4:22). The word *conversation* in the text is an old

English word for "manner of life, behavior, or conduct."[2] The apostle Paul is instructing the people of the Ephesian church to "put off" their former way of life. The "old man" is the natural man apart from Jesus Christ—it's what defined us before salvation. Your former self will be tempted to become angry, resentful, rebellious, hateful, bitter, malicious, unloving, ungodly, unkind, uncaring, thoughtless, jealous, impatient, ungrateful, and worldly. But God says to put off all these things.

Our sinful nature is not eradicated at salvation (don't I wish!), but instead must be mortified (put to death) daily. Paul said in I Corinthians 15:31 "I die daily." Because of our "deceitful lusts," Paul says, our former way of living was corrupt. Paul emphasized this point to the Romans when he said, "For I know that in me (that is, in my flesh,) dwelleth no good thing…O wretched man that I am!" (Romans 7:18, 24). Our old nature *never* gets cleaned up or sanctified, which is why it must be crucified every moment of every day.

You may be thinking, "But that's just the way I am!" Then *change* is needed, and change is precisely what the Holy Spirit is demanding by saying we are not to live as we used to live. In fact, if our actions and habits have not altered dramatically since we made a profession of faith in Jesus Christ, there is reason to doubt the veracity of our salvation experience. "Therefore if any man be in Christ, he is a new creature: old things are passed away; behold, all things are become new" (2 Corinthians 5:17).

Rather than feeling trapped or stuck, operating from an "I can't" attitude, meditate on the Philippians 4:13

exhortation which says, "I can do all things through Christ which strengtheneth me."

## PRINCIPLE 2: CHANGE YOUR THINKING PROCESS

"And be renewed in the spirit of your mind" (Ephesians 4:23). This principle is similarly stated in Romans 12:2a—"And be not conformed to this world: but be ye transformed by the renewing of your mind."

One of the most important transformations that takes place at the moment of salvation is this initial renewing of the mind. It continues throughout the believer's life through the sanctification process. As a believer yields to the Holy Spirit and immerses himself in the Word of God, he is conformed to the image of Jesus Christ.

Satan sees to it that our minds are constantly being bombarded with "the things of this world." Look at one of the old-time movies from back in the 1940s or 50s and then consider what is being shown today. How many people, Christians included, have had the drudges of his world dumped on them via the Internet. Back in the 1970s, we preachers used to encourage parents not to let their children have a tv or phone in their bedroom where they might get into trouble with the eye-gate or the ear-gate. Now most children have in their pocket the ability to indulge both, and more, any time and anywhere. And adults do as well. Indeed, it's much easier for Satan to influence our minds with ungodliness.

Applying this "change your thinking process" with your

spouse, it is seldom wise to indulge in speculation concerning your spouse's motives on anything. An unchecked flight-of-fancy along these lines can only lead to more complex problems. One of Satan's tricks is to get us to try to figure out *why* someone did what they did. Extra-sensory perception, however, is *not* in the list of fruit of the Holy Spirit (Galatians 5:22–23), and there is nothing spiritual about judging another's motives or heart. Let's face it, most of us have a difficult enough time keeping our own motives pure without trying to look into other people's hearts to determine theirs.

I learned a lesson along this line back when my wife and I first started dating. Mary and I were invited to visit a beautiful resort in Virginia and to have dinner with the owner and several other guests. (The head chef at the resort was a member of the church Mary and I were attending in Arlington, Virginia.) Many politicians, congressmen, government officials, and corporations used the resort for special events.

After touring the beautiful grounds, we enjoyed an exquisite dinner. Once we had gone through the buffet line, we found our place among the twenty or so other guests at one of the beautifully decorated tables.

We had no sooner sat down than someone pointed out the proprietor of the place, who, I was told, actually had three earned doctoral degrees. Naturally, I turned to see the man. He was nicely dressed in a sports coat and open-collared shirt, but, as I immediately told Mary, he appeared to be the most stuck-up person I had ever seen. Although he was moving down a buffet line, reaching for the different dishes, he held his shoulders stiffly back, his chin up, his head erect, and he moved with utmost precision. It was plain he wanted all of us to know how important he was.

As he came to sit down, he carried his astuteness and stiffness right to the chair. I looked at this man with the scornful realization that he thought way too much of himself. I had the guy all figured out, and in my heart I had already put him in his place. A few minutes later, however, when someone introduced him to us, he apologized for his stiffness mentioning the back brace he had to wear due to an earlier surgery.

Needless to say, I learned an important lesson about passing judgment on people without knowing the truth. Although it is often said, "Perception is truth," that is not always the case. *Truth* is truth. Remember this in communicating with your husband or wife.

Clearly, right-thinking results in right actions. "For as he thinketh in his heart, so is he" (Proverbs 23:7). Wrong-thinking gives way to wrong actions. The rule of thumb is that we are what we think. Thus anger, malice, bitterness, and depressive thoughts, will usually emanate from a mind given over to self instead of to the Lord. Philippians 2:2–5 provides this instruction: "Fulfil ye my joy, that ye be like-minded, having the same love, being of one accord, of one mind. Let nothing be done through strife or vainglory; but in lowliness of mind let each esteem other better than themselves. Look not every man on his own things, but every man also on the things of others. Let this mind be in you, which was also in Christ Jesus."

The key to a changed thinking process, which is indeed crucial to a lifelong loving marriage, is to have the mind of

Christ. A proper thought life doesn't just happen. It must be sought as tenaciously as you would seek to build your faith, or to be consistent in Bible reading, prayer, or any of the other Christian disciplines. As to what constitutes proper thinking, the Holy Spirit instructs us in Philippians 4:8, "Finally, brethren, whatsoever things are true, whatsoever things are honest, whatsoever things are just, whatsoever things are pure, whatsoever things are lovely, whatsoever things are of good report; if there be any virtue, and if there be any praise, think on these things."

In addition to thinking biblically, it is important to maintain hope for any situation. Husbands and wives are prone to despair when confronted by their spouse's struggles. (The same is true in other relationships, as well, such as when parents are prone to despair when confronted by a path their children are pursuing.) Do not give up. Despair and defeatism have never conquered any mountains. Give yourself and your relationships a chance; learn how to start finding, thinking about, and praising the person's good qualities. Choose to meditate on the positive side of life. If I err, I would rather err thinking on the good side of a person than the bad.

## PRINCIPLE 3: PUT ON THE NEW MAN

The Lord says we are not only to discard, or put *off*, the old nature and to change our thinking process, but we are to put *on* a replacement for that old nature: "And that ye put on the new man, which after God is created in righteousness and true holiness" (Ephesians 4:24). It is not enough to have a list of don'ts—habits that we are trying to undo, such as not showing affection, being indifferent toward our spouse's needs, wasteful spending habits, or wrong reactions and responses. We also need a list of "dos" that ultimately become habitual. God is concerned with a complete transformation in the inner man.

The foundation to these "do's" is the two characteristics found in the verse we just read—the first being *righteousness*. Righteousness in the believer will produce right living. Any other type of living means I resorted back to my old fleshly way that I lived before salvation.

One of the clearest passages of Scripture dealing with the Spirit-filled life is found in Romans 6:11–22. We find in these verses the depth of God's desire that we live and act righteously. Notice particularly the words I have boldfaced:

> Likewise reckon ye also yourselves to be dead indeed unto sin, but alive unto God through Jesus Christ our Lord. Let not sin therefore reign in your mortal body, that ye should obey it in the lusts thereof. Neither yield ye your members as instruments of ***unrighteousness*** unto sin: but yield yourselves unto God, as those that are alive from the dead, and your members as instruments of ***righteousness*** unto God. For sin shall not have dominion over you: for ye are not under the law, but under grace. What then? shall we sin, because we are not under the law, but under grace? God forbid. Know ye not, that to whom ye yield yourselves servants to obey, his servants ye are to whom ye obey; whether of sin unto death, or of obedience unto ***righteousness***? But God be thanked, that ye were the servants of sin, but ye have

> obeyed from the heart that form of doctrine which was delivered you. Being then made free from sin, ye became the servants of ***righteousness***. I speak after the manner of men because of the infirmity of your flesh: for as ye have yielded your members servants to uncleanness and to iniquity unto iniquity; even so now yield your members servants to ***righteousness*** unto holiness. For when ye were the servants of sin, ye were free from ***righteousness***. What fruit had ye then in those things whereof ye are now ashamed? for the end of those things is death. But now being made free from sin, and become servants to God, ye have your fruit unto holiness, and the end everlasting life.

The second characteristic of this "new man," is that he is created in "true holiness," or literally, "holiness of the truth." God is showing that this new man is in juxtaposition to the old man. Instead of the basis of our old nature that is the deceit with which we are born—the new nature is based on truth, and we know "the truth is in Jesus" (Ephesians 4:21). So "holiness of truth" is genuinely "true holiness." In other words, our old nature before salvation is not worked over and cleaned up; rather, we have a new nature emanating from God, the Truth. Holiness means we are set apart to God which is what our Lord does for us when we are saved. As we grow in our walk with the Lord, we choose to be set apart (holy) not only positionally (which is God's work) through salvation, but also practically. This means we choose to continue to be holy, which includes purity in our thoughts, our words, and our actions. Please keep in mind that our "new man" is not a re-do of the old—it is not our old man "cleaned up and starting over."

So, these two characteristics—righteousness and true holiness—become God's description of who we are in Christ. They are together the essence of God's character, and hence, what He wants for believers. "But as he which hath called you is holy, so be ye holy in all manner of conversation; Because it is written, Be ye holy; for I am holy" (1 Peter 1:15–16).

How often we find when attempting to resolve conflicts—especially marital or family conflicts—that these characteristics are sorely lacking in our communication. We get too concerned about our feelings, our pride, our hurt, our anger, or the injustice done us; and we often demonstrate a mixture of uncontrolled emotions. We each need to reflect on our overall conduct and behavior any time there is a problem needing resolution.

A person's pride and ego are great hindrances to problem solving—not just with the family, but in any relationship. When it comes to "righteousness and true holiness," we should make Christ alone our final standard. Often, in our present culture of Christianity, many churches and Christians appear to get as close to the world in their standards, habits, and music as the unsaved crowd. Our goal for our homes and churches is not to see how we can blend in with the world; rather, it is to be a living testimony governed by the Bible in the pursuit of righteousness and true holiness. This pursuit will guide our steps as we seek to strengthen our marriages.

THREE

# The Truth of the Matter

Lying is the icy water that freezes communication. Not only is it a sin against God, but it paves the way for distrust between the communicators.

## PRINCIPLE 4: PUT AWAY LYING

"Wherefore putting away lying…" (Ephesians 4:25). "I'm sorry, I won't be home for dinner tonight. I have to work late," is a message many wives have received. Sometimes what the husband means is that he is unwilling to go home to a nagging wife or to resolve some difficult situation. He has seized an excuse to postpone the inevitable.

Then, there is the wife who purchases two new outfits at the store but is waiting for the "right time" to release this bulletin. She tells herself she is not actually *lying*, because she fully intends to break the news to her husband *sometime.*

Where do lies originate? And, what constitutes a lie? John 8:44 is clear: "Ye are of your father the devil, and the lusts of your father ye will do. He was a murderer from the beginning, and abode not in the truth, because there is no truth in him. When he speaketh a lie, he speaketh of his own: for he is a liar, and the father of it." Lies originate with their father—the devil. He deceives you into believing that deceit would be more advantageous for you than the truth. So, you are deceived into deceiving.

A lie is communication based on deceit. That communication can be via word or action. The root of a lie is deceit. We may outright speak a lie, or we may lie by withholding truth. We may lie by staging a cover-up, no matter how simple or harmless it may seem to us. Half-truths are whole lies.

Never resort to lying. Lying is the coward's escape route, indicating not only a lack of faith in God to work through truth and repentance, but also a profound lack of character. Additionally, lying tears apart the very foundation of communication. Any kind of family discussion will be fruitless if the participants are predisposed to lying.

Jeremiah 17:9 instructs, "The heart is deceitful above all things, and desperately wicked: who can know it?" Deceit and lying come easily to all of us, because our own hearts are deceitful. That's why we can't trust our hearts—we must trust the Holy Spirit to teach us truth and to teach us how to tell and live the truth. The psalmists knew this truth: "Deliver my soul, O Lord, from lying lips, and from a deceitful tongue" (Psalm 120:2). "For the mouth of the wicked and the mouth of the deceitful are opened against me: they have spoken against me with a lying tongue" (Psalm 109:2).

Once the first lie has been told it becomes much easier, and even seems necessary, for the second lie to be told. A spouse living with a secret is easily deceived into thinking that in order to protect his or her secret, there is no option other than being untruthful. The spouse may be protecting an affair, a drug habit, a liaison, spending habits, or other secret sins.

The thought process goes something like this: "If she finds out the truth, my wife would ___________." Fear of the consequences that would result if the truth were known often deceitfully justifies in one's mind the telling and living of a lie.

We have all lied at some time throughout our lives. And we've all been lied to. The remembrance of the pain and consequences from both sides of the lie should serve as strong reminders to *never* demonstrate this kind of deceitful and deceptive character. Lying never succeeds in building a good relationship or in healing communication.

Trust is earned. Once a spouse finds out the hard way you have been lying, it is a long road to rebuild that sacred, mutual trust. It is incumbent upon the those who were doing the lying to prove they are now trustworthy, rather than demanding to be trusted again. This may be a little longer process than you thought. Of course, the best action is to not lie in the first place—to not chance losing the trust of your spouse by "hiding the truth," lying.

Is there something you need to talk to your spouse,

children, parents, or friend about? The best time is now. The only thing worse than telling a lie is living a lie.

The genuine antidote to lying is the next principle: "speak the truth."

## PRINCIPLE 5: SPEAK THE TRUTH

We find in Isaiah 1:16b–17a a distinct difference between good and evil and what to do about it: "Cease to do evil; Learn to do well." It is not enough to stop doing evil—we need to replace it with doing well. This is an example of God's put off/put on cycle that we have already seen in Ephesians 4:22–24, where we were instructed to put off the old man and put on the new man. We are to replace the bad we put off, with good that we put on.

It is not difficult to imagine what God would teach us to replace lying with. We put off lying, replacing it with speaking and living truth.: "Wherefore putting away lying, speak every man truth with his neighbour: for we are members one of another" (Ephesians 4:25).

Being a truth teller is liberating for the soul. The Bible says, "And ye shall know the truth, and the truth shall make you free" (John 8:32). And it's all about the Lord Jesus Christ: "If the Son therefore shall make you free, ye shall be free indeed" (John 8:36). For those of us who have received Jesus Christ as our personal Saviour, there is nothing like the true freedom we have found in the Son of God. As we noted above, He *is* "the way, the truth, and the life" (John 14:6), and He is also the one through whom we receive the power and the strength to be like Him—to tell the truth. "I can do all things through Christ which strengtheneth me" (Philippians 4:13).

Put away lying. Speak and live truth. Make this a matter of fervent prayer and faith. Every time you are tempted to present deception as if it were truth, ask the Lord to strengthen you, giving you courage to speak and live the truth. And, every time you allow Him to present truth through you, you will be strengthened to tell the truth the next time.

Husbands and wives should speak the truth in every area. Are you truthful with your spouse in the matters of finances, thoughts, opinions, children, work, friends, church, convictions, and relationships? There is no area of life that you should live secretly from your spouse—you are to be one flesh. Hide nothing.

FOUR

# The Daily Grind

I'm intrigued by yard sales and garage sales where people sell their stockpiled trash to someone else who considers it treasure. The mentality behind this "treasure exchange" has always eluded me. These newly-acquired treasures, after a couple of months, are often placed in an attic and stockpiled—along with other gems—toward a future sale.

Sad but true, many families use the same technique with their problems, stockpiling them until the "attic" is full. Unfortunately, by the time the attic becomes full, many couples and families have already deemed it too late to free themselves of their hoard.

Problems, when ignored, can accumulate like snowflakes. Individually, they may feel light, and you believe you can handle them. But together, they build, forming a solid mass that can overwhelm and crush you.

## PRINCIPLE 6: WORK OUT PROBLEMS DAILY

"Be ye angry, and sin not: let not the sun go down upon your wrath" (Ephesians 4:26). Husbands may say, "Well if that's the way she's going to be, I'll show her. I'll sleep on the couch tonight!" Alternately, a wife might give the silent treatment to a husband who has frustrated her. Sleeping on the couch and giving the silent treatment are two stockpiling techniques, and they prove that you have a communication breakdown. You must believe me, your home life can be sweet if you decide to work on it, especially if you follow this principle.

Too many Christian couples go to bed angry with each other. Rather than resolving their conflicts before the day ends as Ephesians 4:26 teaches, they allow it to linger. Yet, absolutely nothing is resolved or improved by ignoring the problem or by pretending it will go away—ever.

The Christian life only works when lived according to biblical principles, not according to feelings. *Your feelings* may dictate that you go to bed with your marital or family problems unresolved, but *God's principle* teaches "Let not the sun go down upon your wrath" (Ephesians 4:26b). If you've ever followed your feelings, so that you slept on the couch rather than resolving the conflict, you realized that the problem was still there when you woke up. Absolutely nothing is resolved or improved by ignoring the problem or by pretending it will go away.

The problem may lie beyond the family unit, with a

church member, a co-worker, or a fellow student, or neighbor. If the grievance has not been biblically settled through courteous, Christ-like conversation with that person, now is the time. Make an effort toward this end immediately.

Having a successful marital relationship, like any church relationship, means giving immediate attention to the problem. Realize though, that, while there will always be people in church who may choose to walk away from a problem rather than dealing with it, you *cannot* walk away from your spouse. Staying in love for life can only be achieved by two people who are committed to doing the will of God by resolving all problems, *daily*.

It's easy to shrug off an offense with the thought that you weren't the one who started the problem in the first place. Biblically, however, it really is nonconsequential who started a problem. The point is that there *is* a problem. "Therefore if thou bring thy gift to the altar, and there rememberest that thy brother hath aught against thee; Leave there thy gift before the altar, and go thy way; first be reconciled to thy brother, and then come and offer thy gift" (Matthew 5:23–24). Jesus dealt with this idea again in Matthew 18:15: "Moreover if thy brother shall trespass against thee, go and tell him his fault between thee and him alone: if he shall hear thee, thou hast gained thy brother." Assuming I can't let love cover the other person's offense, it is my responsibility to go to that brother or sister—and there is no closer brother or sister than your spouse.

The fact that a problem exists with your awareness means you have the God-given responsibility to seek to resolve it immediately. Whether the offense occurred at home, church, school, work, or play, it is your responsibility to seek a resolution. And if the offence occurred in your marriage, resolving it is essential for continued marital communication.

FIVE

# Speaking of the Devil

"The devil made me do it," is an expression often heard when a fallen brother explains why he has sinned. The devil never makes us do anything! He may suggest something to us, but we make the decision to actually do it. Husbands and wives need to identify, confront, and admit their sins, instead of passing them over to the devil.

The good news is that we who are saved have the Holy Spirit of God living inside us, giving us the power *not* to sin: "Greater is he that is in you, than he that is in the world" (1 John 4:4). Jesus Christ is omnipotent; Satan is not. If we follow Paul's admonition in Galatians 5:16 to "walk in the Spirit," only then will we realize that we have the power and anointing of God to conquer any temptation coming our way. God provides the way to bear and escape *every* temptation: "There hath no temptation taken you but such as is common to man: but God is faithful, who will not suffer you to be tempted above that ye are able; but will with the temptation also make a way to escape, that ye may be able to bear it" (1 Corinthians 10:13).

## PRINCIPLE 7: GUARD AGAINST SATAN

Because communication is vital for the success of the home, it will be a major focus of Satan's attacks. Thus, Ephesians 4:27 warns, "Neither give place to the devil."

"To give place to is to get out of the way of, to allow free scope to; and therefore to give an occasion or advantage to anyone."[3] The essence of this communication principle is to *make sure the devil has no room to advance his cause in or through your life*. Because Christ is to be the head of every home, we must never allow Satan a foothold in our lives. Peter admonished us, "Be sober, be vigilant; because your adversary the devil, as a roaring lion, walketh about, seeking whom he may devour: Whom resist steadfast in the faith" (1 Peter 5:8–9).

The devil's ploy is to tempt us to shun communication (or at least to put it off), to ignore problems, to fail in understanding, to exercise impatience, and to be uncaring. He also encourages us to demonstrate a quick, sharp, caustic manner with our family, to be unloving, proud, selfish, irresponsible, angry, unforgiving, and insensitive to the needs of our spouse. Let these descriptive words, as a warning signal, open your eyes—they are marks of a fleshly, carnal person. They are certainly not indicative of a godly, loving spouse.

Most of us need a daily reminder that we in fact are in a war just as real and devastating as any war any nation has ever seen. The devil has put land mines all around our pathways, just waiting for us to get off course. As the "prince of the power of the air" (Ephesians 2:2), he bombards us with regular attacks designed to dethrone the Lord from our lives.

Because we wrestle "against principalities, against powers, against the rulers of the darkness of this world, against spiritual wickedness in high places" (Ephesians 6:12), God provided us with all the resources we need in the way of armor (Ephesians 6:13–17). We also have the Word of God and the Holy Spirit to guide and empower us so that we are without excuse for not having victory. The difficulty we have in resolving problems is not the lack of resources; but rather our pride and hurt feelings.

Most of us admit we are sinners with deceitful and wicked hearts—in a kind of detached way. Yet, we somehow seldom see that we could possibly be at fault when an argument or disagreement arises. Often we don't see ourselves as even being *part* of the problem! And when we are bold enough to admit being part of the problem, we often excuse our own sinful behavior by saying it was caused by our spouse.

Someone else's (your spouse's) bad behavior cannot make you sin by responding with your own attack. If your response to another's action is sinful, it is because you have succumbed to the tricks and temptations of the devil.

It is important to keep in mind that as you continue on your journey toward a loving marriage and godly home, Satan will not be smiling with his arms folded, approving of your right choices. On the contrary, every time you seek to do something for God, Satan becomes more determined to wrest the control. Keep in mind our Commander-in-Chief's order by which we opened this principle: "Neither give place to the devil" (Ephesians 4:27). Never succumb to Satan—resist every time.

## PRINCIPLE 8: QUIT STEALING

The next verse in Ephesians 4 reads, "Let him that stole steal no more" (Ephesians 4:28). Most Christians, when they read this passage of Scripture, immediately skip to the following verse, thinking that since they are not in the habit of going into a store and slipping something under their coat, it does not apply to them. Stealing merchandise is only one of many kinds of stealing. We will address two additional types related to marriage:

First, there is **stealing time.** One of the worst methods of stealing is the time spouses steal from each other. It is easy for one or the other to think their time is more valuable than their spouse's. This is particularly true in homes where both husband and wife work. At the conclusion of a long day, both are tired; consequently, after a quick bite to eat, they begin making independent plans for the evening. Often, the husband props himself before the television while the wife does the dishes and makes sure the children have done their homework.

The only way to stop this practice of stealing is to start planning and scheduling time together. Otherwise, the distance between you grows. Families should plan time together to communicate, to play, to work, to go to church, to love, to share, to relate to one another, and to have a time for family devotions. A "house" is a place where people of the same family dwell, each pursuing his own interests. A Christian "home" is the place where family members spend time together, serving the Lord, *and each other.*

A second kind of theft is **stealing affection.** It is extremely important that husbands and wives be consistently on guard against stealing affection from someone other than their own spouse. Keep the flames of marital bliss kindled so the warmth of love permeates the home, and time will not be needed later to stamp out flirtations smoldering on the side.

Even a casual reading of the Book of Proverbs should be warning enough to exercise discipline over the flesh. Proverbs 6:32–33 warns, "But whoso committeth adultery with a woman lacketh understanding: he that doeth it destroyeth his own soul. A wound and dishonor shall he get; and his reproach shall not be wiped away." Flirtations will not only destroy your marriage, they will destroy *you*!

We are reminded of this principle throughout the Bible. Hebrews 13:4 clearly states, "Marriage is honourable in all, and the bed undefiled: but whoremongers and adulterers God will judge."

The antidote for any type of stealing is to work: "but rather let him labour, working with his hands the thing which is good, that he may have to give to him that needeth" (Ephesians 4:28b). To keep from stealing time, affection, love, or property, learn to invest time in service to others, especially those within your family.

So, ask yourself: If I have been stealing time from my spouse, what is the antidote? What "labor" can I perform to give him or her time, rather than stealing it? If I have been stealing affection, what is the antidote? What "labor" can I perform to give affection to my spouse, rather than to someone else?

Follow God's put off/put on principle, and your life will be turned into one of giving, rather than one of taking.

SIX

# Talking Points

A married couple is comprised of two distinct individuals whose backgrounds may be polar opposites. As is the case with my Mary and me, one of you may have come to know Christ as a child, while the other was saved as an adult. Or, one may have been saved after marriage, while the other has yet to receive Christ as Saviour. One may have grown up in a Christian home, while the other grew up in a home where Christ was not known or honored.

In every case where there is at least one Christian spouse involved, it is possible and necessary for communication to be Spirit-filled. "Let no corrupt communication proceed out of your mouth, but that which is good to the use of edifying, that it may minister grace unto the hearers" (Ephesians 4:29).

## PRINCIPLE 9: USE DISCRETION WHEN COMMUNICATING

Have you ever watched a reality police show? When the police officer shows up at the door of a couple's house to handle a domestic dispute, the couple typically wastes no time berating each other with ungodly and abusive language. I believe that this is sadly the case in many Christian homes, as well.

While communication in your home may not involve this extreme display of offensive language, still seek to be careful and discreet when talking to your spouse (or anyone, for that matter). The psalmist said, "Set a watch, O LORD, before my mouth; keep the door of my lips" (Psalm 141:3).

When seeking to use discretion in your communication, remember that every spouse (because of our corrupt nature) has been guilty of some (or many) thoughts, words, or deeds which do not bear repeating. It is unwise and hurtful to flippantly bring up past issues and mistakes that have already been confessed to the Lord and, as applicable, resolved as a couple.

Like you, I have some things in my past that I am particularly thankful that even God has forgotten about—"And their sins and iniquities will I remember no more" (Hebrews 10:17). These types of confessed, past mistakes should not be rehearsed or discussed repeatedly.

While some spouses look at their past with great regret and remorse, others seem to glory in their former way of living. Instead of being offended when someone else references past mistakes, this type of spouse may freely discuss personal issues and relationships from the past. In each of these situations, God instructs, "Let no corrupt communication proceed out of your mouth." The word *corrupt* here has the connotation of unwholesomeness or rottenness—as in rotten fruit or smelly fish. Don't bring back the rotten smell of former mistakes. If past sins have been confessed biblically, leave them in the past and under the blood of Jesus Christ. It is hurtful to your spouse when you continue to bring up a past life that involved sin against God and your spouse.

James 3:6–8 warns of the importance of guarding our words: "And the tongue is a fire, a world of iniquity: so is the tongue among our members, that it defileth the whole body, and setteth on fire the course of nature; and it is set on fire of hell. For every kind of beasts, and of birds, and of serpents, and of things in the sea, is tamed, and hath been tamed of mankind: But the tongue can no man tame; it is an unruly evil, full of deadly poison."

## PRINCIPLE 10: BUILD UP RATHER THAN TEAR DOWN

The childhood verse, "Sticks and stones may break my bones but words will never hurt me," could not be further from the truth. Most of us have been there. We can recall instances where being struck repeatedly with a stick would have been much less painful than receiving a verbal lashing that left us in shreds emotionally.

And the problem is, it doesn't only hurt us—man's sinful nature wants to return evil for evil. We pass the lashing on.

Every communication within your marriage should be "good to the use of edifying, that it may minister grace unto the hearers" (Ephesians 4:29). To edify is to build up. This again is part of the put off/put on dynamic each couple must exercise in developing good communication. We must put off offensive communication and put on edifying communication.

Be intentional in building up one another. A kind way of expressing criticism, if you feel you must criticize it, is to sandwich the criticism between positive statements. For instance, "Honey, I really appreciate the hard work you do in providing for our family. I know you don't mean anything by it, but is there any way you could pick up your dirty socks? It would help in keeping our bedroom tidy, and I would really appreciate it." Choose your words carefully. One ill-chosen word or phrase can destroy a month of loving deeds.

Interestingly enough, the ability (or lack of it) to control the tongue is one method of discerning whether there is substance to a person's faith. James 1:26 states, "If any man among you seem to be religious, and bridleth not his tongue, but deceiveth his own heart, this man's religion is vain."

The truth is, many bad attitudes and problems in the home could be eliminated if all family members spoke kindly to each other. Pause right now and think of ten positive things that could be said toward building up your spouse or another family member. Write them down, and begin using them in your conversations.

It does no good to win a battle of words but lose your family in the process. Determine to minister grace through your speech to your spouse.

## PRINCIPLE 11: COMMUNICATE WHILE FILLED WITH THE SPIRIT

I had been saved fifteen months when I was called into the ministry and went off to Bible college. I remember, as a freshman, walking across campus with a junior, who later turned out to be a close friend. He asked me, "Are you filled with the Spirit?"

Well, during my fifteen months of Christianity, I had heard that Pentecostals claimed to be filled with the Holy Spirit and that they believed they proved it by speaking in tongues. I proudly responded to the young man, "No way. I've never been filled with the Spirit!" It didn't take long for me to learn that being filled with the Spirit is God's plan for *all* Christians. While the Holy Spirit permanently indwells each person the moment he or she receives Christ as Saviour from sin, we must each choose to walk in and be filled with the Holy Spirit. So, how is a person filled with the Holy Spirit, since it is something God wants all of us to be?

First, we must confess our sins to God. It is impossible to be filled with the Holy Spirit or to walk in the Spirit with unconfessed sin in our lives. First John 1:9 says, "If we confess our sins, he is faithful and just to forgive us our sins, and to cleanse us from all unrighteousness." Remember, we can never prosper by covering our sins. God makes that clear in Proverbs 28:13: "He that covereth his sins shall not prosper: but whoso confesseth and forsaketh them shall have mercy." All known sin must be confessed to God before anyone can expect to walk in the Spirit.

Second, you must dedicate your life completely to God.

Paul exhorted Christians to "yield yourselves unto God, as those that are alive from the dead, and your members as instruments of righteousness unto God" (Romans 6:13). Again Paul urged, "I beseech you therefore, brethren, by the mercies of God, that ye present your bodies a living sacrifice, holy, acceptable unto God, which is your reasonable service" (Romans 12:1).

This is not a game to God. If we expect to have the blessings of the Lord, we must dedicate our whole being to Him. Absolute dedication is a prerequisite for being filled with the Holy Spirit. Jesus said to His disciples in Luke 9:23: "If any man will come after me, let him deny himself, and take up his cross daily, and follow me."

Third, you must ask the Lord for His filling. That is simply praying to God, asking Him to fill you with His Holy Spirit. Jesus promised, "And whatsoever ye shall ask in my name, that will I do, that the Father may be glorified in the Son. If ye shall ask any thing in my name, I will do it" (John 14:13–14).

The filling of the Holy Spirit is not a once and for all action, as some have implied. Neither is it to be thought of as something designed for a single purpose like soulwinning or teaching Sunday school. Don't get me wrong; being filled with the Holy Spirit is mandatory in order to be a good soulwinner, teacher, or preacher. But that's not all. Rather, God says, "And be not drunk with wine, wherein is excess; but be filled with the Spirit" (Ephesians 5:18).

The idea is to be *continually* filled with the Holy Spirit of God. Paul told the people of the church of Galatia that they were to "walk in the Spirit" (Galatians 5:25). We are to be both continually filled and continually directed by God's Holy Spirit. Absolutely nothing should be done through the power and energy of the flesh, for to do so would be to estrange yourself from God.

Because of a lack of knowledge, some Bible believing Christians suspect that walking in the Spirit is superstitious, fanatical, or impossible—something reserved for the emotional crowd of which they have no part. But *every* Christian must be concerned to not grieve the Holy Spirit or in any way to bring reproach upon the name of our Lord. Simply put, we are to stop grieving or bringing grief to the Holy Spirit of God. Ephesians 4:30 says, "And grieve not the holy Spirit of God, whereby ye are sealed unto the day of redemption."

Failure to control our flesh definitely grieves the Holy Spirit. "This I say then, Walk in the Spirit, and ye shall not fulfil the lust of the flesh" (Galatians 5:16). Walking in the Spirit and not fulfilling the lust of the flesh is the only way to *not* grieve His Holy Spirit. But this doctrine is one that may seem easier said than done.

My experience in counseling hundreds of couples throughout the years is that the typical couple with marital problems thinks that the marriage is about *their* happiness, *their* peace of mind, *their* welfare. Many a husband or wife has been quick to point out the other's problems which are causing them to experience personal grief and heartache, without any consideration as to what God thinks, or to the grief He may be experiencing because of their own behavior. So, a breakdown in communication between the couple signals that there is also a breakdown in someone's relationship with the Holy Spirit.

In communicating, our whole countenance, body, voice, and heart should reflect the Lord Jesus Christ. Before speaking to your spouse, pray for the filling of the Holy Spirit! This means as you get up in the morning, acknowledge God's presence and ask for His filling. It is a continual walk with the Lord, yielding our all to Him.

Husbands who are filled with the Holy Spirit make better communicators, lovers, and leaders. They are also more successful fathers. And by the way, if there is any doubt in your mind regarding your walk with the Lord, all you have to do is humbly and honestly ask a family member how you are doing. I warn you though, if you are not prepared for a brutally honest answer and ready to confess your sin and ask the Holy Spirit to fill you, you may not want to try this exercise.

Wives who are filled with the Holy Spirit make better encouragers, communicators, and mothers. Every woman should ask God for the filling of the Holy Spirit as she begins each day. Walking in the Spirit can add meaning to many of the mundane activities that sometimes fill a woman's day. Housework, meal preparation, caring for a family—all of this and more, when done with the filling of the Holy Spirit, can honor God and be a transforming influence in the life of a family.

It might be good to pause and ask yourself, "Am I a Spirit-filled communicator?" The only way any of us will experience a lifetime of love and meaningful communication in our marriage is with help from the Lord.

God never intended for Spirit-filled communication to be something mystical or only for the "super-spiritual." Again, the steps to being filled with the Spirit are simple: Confess all known sin to God (Proverbs 28:13; 1 John 1:9), dedicate your life completely to God, and call on the Lord now and ask Him for His filling. Make it your daily habit.

SEVEN

# Get Rid of These Things

"Search me, O God, and know my heart: try me, and know my thoughts: And see if there be any wicked way in me, and lead me in the way everlasting." (Psalm 139:23–24)

Our Ephesians 4 passage continues with a list of things we should remove or "put off" from our marriages. As a spouse, we should constantly ask the Holy Spirit to search us, showing us areas in our lives that are hurting our relationships with not only the Lord, but with our spouse and other family members, as well.

## PRINCIPLE 12: PUT AWAY BITTERNESS

"Let all bitterness…be put away from you" (Ephesians 4:31).

In this portion of Scripture, we are admonished to put away any bitterness in our lives. Hebrews 12:15 also warns, "Lest any root of bitterness springing up trouble you, and thereby many be defiled." Bitterness effectually kills good communication, and it spills over in every other area of life.

The truth is, the only person bitterness really hurts is you! If *you* allow someone to make you so mad that a root starts spreading in your life, then *you* are the one who suffers the effects of it. When anger is improperly dealt with, or not dealt with at all, it will eventually turn into bitterness; and when bitterness grows its deep and tangled roots, it could linger for a lifetime.

"She'll pay for this," "I'll get him," or "I'll never forget that," are statements emanating from a bitter heart. Anger always precedes bitterness, and when not immediately dealt with, it results in bitterness. It's like a festering sore that stays active, oozing out rottenness and poison. When a person reacts with anger or self-pity because of another's unkind words or deeds, bitterness often sets in.

To get rid of bitterness, we must practice forgiveness. In chapter 8, we will study this quality of forgiveness in depth, as it is mandatory to a loving marriage. For now, understand that the root of bitterness spreads through your whole life, choking emotions and relationships. Don't give bitterness place in your life—put it away. Your life and marriage are worth it!

## PRINCIPLE 13: PUT AWAY WRATH

The second item in Paul's list of things that need to be put away is wrath. Wrath can be defined as "a strong passion or emotion of the mind"[4] or "a violent outbreak of anger, anger forthwith boiling up and soon subsiding again."[5] This emotion, though God-given, has its proper place. While

Christians should display great wrath and hatred for the devil, they should not display it for one another. In our marriages, we must learn to control our emotions, rather than allowing our emotions to control us. Any person can be dominated by negative emotions; only the Christian can practice the self-control which springs from the Holy Spirit's indwelling and empowering.

A wrathful spirit will impede the flow of good communication. Wrath is not to be vented; it should be restrained and confessed to God.

## PRINCIPLE 14: PUT AWAY ANGER

Next on the list of characteristics to put away is anger. "Let all…anger…be put away from you" (Ephesians 4:31).

Anger should be banned from your communication with your spouse. You may come from a long line of fighters, from parents who communicated mostly through harsh arguments. You may have learned to communicate the same way. If so, this principle is very important for you to grasp.

If you are in the habit of quarreling, fussing, or fighting, break from that tradition and put it far from you. You have to say to yourself, "I can change, and by God's grace, I will." The next time the children's toys litter the floor, dinner is late, or you didn't get the response you were looking for, remember—anger is not the correct response.

I was in a recent couples' conference where one man who had been married over fifty years was asked the "secret" of his marriage. He responded, "I didn't get married to fight, but to love." That's sound reasoning.

Often people respond in anger when they feel violated, unappreciated (or underappreciated), hurt, or spoken down to. It is easy to justify in our minds that "the only way to respond to this fire is with fire." There is, however, a better and more biblical way, and that is to respond with love and kindness. It is entirely possible that you misunderstood their intentions, as bad as they may have been.

A fight doesn't necessarily begin with the one who "started it." While he or she may have said something that triggered a response, who is responsible for what response is given? When your spouse accuses or belittles you, is he or she the one who "starts the fight"? Or are you?

We each have a choice when someone "pushes our buttons." We can respond in kind to their accusation, or we can respond in love and self-control.

All spouses over the course of a marriage say many things that could be taken wrongly (or rightly, for that matter) as hurtful accusations or motive judgments. The couples who get through those times are the ones in which one or both spouses choose to be responsible for their own thoughts, actions, and responses. When you respond through the power and with the fruit of the Holy Spirit (Galatians 5:22–23), the argument will quickly turn to biblical communication. As Proverbs 15:1 says, "A soft answer turneth away wrath: but grievous words stir up anger."

If my spouse, or anyone else, does or says something that stirs up heated emotions in me, I am to exercise self-discipline and restraint in my response. Their action does not give me a license to respond in kind no matter how I may feel.

## PRINCIPLE 15: PUT AWAY CLAMOR

"Clamor" is an old word, denoting an outcry and implying an immediate burst of anger. You've seen this demonstrated from those who just seem to blow up when things don't go their way. So many marriages take a giant step backward when the husband or wife overreacts to any given situation. There is no place in a godly home for this kind of behavior.

A man may awake in the morning and decide to treat his wife by allowing her a little extra sleep. Quietly, he steals down the stairs and prepares his own breakfast and sack lunch. He returns upstairs to gently kiss her goodbye. After a long day at the office, he stops at the florist for a bunch of daisies, which he gives to his wife with a kiss when he returns home. Because of the special treatment she has received that day, the wife has a succulent meal awaiting her loving leader. After their family devotions and playtime with the children, the two decide to retire for the evening.

The husband carries his shoes and suit coat into their bedroom only to find the bed still unmade and his pajamas where he left them that morning. Barely able to believe his eyes, he drops his shoes and suit coat, and with his arms crossed and head shaking in disgust, he bursts out, "Barbara (he never uses sweet language when he's furious, but always calls her by her first name), what have you been doing all day? If you weren't so lazy, this room would be cleaned by now!"

With this one clamorous outburst, the husband destroyed every bit of love he had fostered during the prior twenty-four hour period. In fact, now the wife might have to deliberate long and hard to recognize *anything* good in her husband.

When situations arise that you may not like, sometimes the best thing to do is to take a deep breath, count to a million, and hug your spouse. Or, simply ask for a clarification and give your spouse the benefit of the doubt. Then, lovingly try to rectify the situation. Love still covers a multitude of sins (1 Peter 4:8).

## PRINCIPLE 16: PUT AWAY EVIL SPEAKING

If couples are to develop good communication, then they will have to follow the apostle Paul's admonition to the church at Ephesus and put away "evil speaking" (Ephesians 4:31). The words *evil speaking* are from the one Greek word, *blasphemia*. The English word *blasphemy* is a transliteration of this Greek word. *Blasphemia* itself is a combination of two words, one meaning "to injure" and the other meaning "speech."[6] The word *blasphemia*, then, conveys the idea of injurious speech, evil speaking, or reviling. It has also been translated "slander." Do not revile each other or hold each other in contempt for failing to meet all personal needs or expectations

Be careful, because you are accountable to God for the things that you say and the way in which you say them. A good rule of thumb for using appropriate words can be found in Philippians 4:8, which we have already looked at: "Finally, brethren, whatsoever things are true, whatsoever things are honest, whatsoever things are just, whatsoever things are pure, whatsoever things are lovely, whatsoever things are of good report; if there be any virtue, and if there be any praise, think on these things."

James said it clearly: "Even so the tongue is a little member, and boasteth great things. Behold, how great a matter a little fire kindleth! And the tongue is a fire, a world of iniquity: so is the tongue among our members, that it defileth the whole body, and setteth on fire the course of nature; and it is set on fire of hell....But the tongue can no man tame" (James 3:5–6, 8a).

## PRINCIPLE 17: PUT AWAY MALICE

Last on Paul's list of things to be put away is malice (Ephesians 4:31). The word *malice* connotes a bad or wicked character. When a person desires to hurt someone else, he is harboring malice in his heart.

Malice stems from a nature that is totally selfish, unloving, and uncaring. Malice has everything to do with the heart. Jeremiah 17:9 tells that our hearts are "deceitful above all things, and desperately wicked; who can know it?"

There is probably nothing that will crush the communication process with your spouse any more than malice. Ask the Holy Spirit to examine your heart for malice, lay it at the feet of Jesus, and ask God to change you from the inside out.

EIGHT

# Tender Hearts

It has been said "A happy marriage requires two elements: two people who know each other thoroughly and two people who accept each other completely." The key to achieving this kind of relationship is through kind, tenderhearted communication and ever-ready forgiveness.

## PRINCIPLE 18: BE KIND TO EACH OTHER

I'll never forget the Christian mobile home park Mary and I lived in while I was in school preparing for ministry. When our son, Troy, was old enough, we often took him to play on the swing sets and slides in the park's play area. Right there on the playground was a large wooden sign that read, "Be Ye Kind." I always thought that was a good lesson to teach young people every time they felt the urge to knock someone else off the swing set so they could swing!

Ephesians 4:32 commands us, "And be ye kind one to another..." Kindness is the ambience that should pervade every discussion. Is there anyone who does not flourish under kindness?

A home without kindness will soon come unglued. "Please pass the potatoes...Thank you," will produce a more desirable reaction than simply "Give me the potatoes." Similarly, as I would try to speak to our son when he lived in our home, "Troy, would you please take the dog outside?" is kinder than "Get that dog out of here!"

Mary regularly asks me, "Can I get you anything?" Although I know I don't deserve to be waited on, she doesn't hesitate to ask this question, just as she did about five minutes ago. I am now sitting here with my computer on my lap trying to think what I can do to return her kindness. Kindness is a great investment that goes a long way.

Let's face it, attitude is everything in the service of our Lord. If I am not kind and gracious to my spouse, I won't be to my Lord either. More times than not, a servant's heart is needed. Jesus said, "Whosoever will be great among you, let him be your minister; And whosoever will be chief among you, let him be your servant" (Matthew 20:26–27).

If problems are to be profitably discussed and resolved, there must be an atmosphere of kindness. Someone has said, "Kindness is Spirit-imparted goodness of heart. It is the very opposite of malice."[7]

Our source of kindness is God Himself, who is good

and kind. He desires to give us love that is made known by its kindness. "Charity suffereth long, and is kind" (1 Corinthians 13:4).

## PRINCIPLE 19: BE TENDERHEARTED

What person comes to your mind when you think of the characteristic of tenderheartedness? It is never a self-serving person, but one who shows gentle, obvious concern for others. Phil Kitchings, the longest serving deacon at the Fairfax Baptist Temple and a dear friend of mine, has for years demonstrated this lifestyle toward his dear wife. About ten years ago, as the result of a serious surgery, she awoke with some limitations. Though she is still the loving wife she always was, Phil has had opportunity to demonstrate what a tender heart truly is. Tenderheartedness doesn't show up in only words, but in actions—it is made known throughout your whole being.

I have always thought that Jesus demonstrated this so well when, seeking to settle a dispute among the disciples, He "called a little child unto him, and set him in the midst of them, And said, Verily I say unto you, Except ye be converted, and become as little children, ye shall not enter into the kingdom of heaven. Whosoever therefore shall humble himself as this little child, the same is greatest in the kingdom of heaven" (Matthew 18:2–4).

Jesus obviously could have "fought fire with fire," pointing out the proud spirits in His disciples. He could have told them that none of them deserved to be considered the greatest. But He chose rather to demonstrate tenderheartedness toward His self-serving disciples, teaching them through a convicting third-person illustration, rather than through a pointed lecture.

Tenderheartedness thinks through the emotions of other people. How will they be able to hear what I am trying to communicate? Would my first intuition hurt them if I spoke what first came to my mind? How can I soften it so I can speak tenderly to their heart?

## PRINCIPLE 20: FORGIVE ONE ANOTHER

The three words, "I forgive you" are among the sweetest in the English language, while the act of forgiveness is the velvet ribbon adorning and cushioning the marriage package. The word *forgive* in the text encompasses a broader significance than simply that of forgiving sin. One commentator explains it this way: "…to do a favor to, do something agreeable or pleasant to one, to show one's self gracious, benevolent, to forgive in the sense of treating the offending party graciously.[8]

The command is to be "…forgiving one another, even as God for Christ's sake hath forgiven you" (Ephesians 4:32). In order to know how to forgive as God forgives, we must get a glimpse of what God's forgiveness really is.

God's forgiveness towards us is free: He forgives us far more than we can ever be called upon to forgive others. God forgives us in Christ: out of Christ He is, in virtue of His holiness and justice, a consuming fire; but in Him, He is long-suffering, abundant in mercy, and ready to forgive.[9]

All of us who have been married any length of time should

value forgiveness highly. We have been forgiven far more than we realize. I have always been most thankful for a loving wife who has been so gracious to quickly forgive me of offenses.

Our goal when offenses occur in our relationships should not be to declare a "winner." Rather, it is to be reconciled. Reconciliation should be sought after every offense. As we seek reconciliation, it is important that we focus on our spouse's feelings, rather than our own. Choosing meaningful, biblical words will help us in this way.

Notice the difference between two possible roads to reconciliation:

1. "I'm sorry." This short, common colloquialism puts the focus on how *I feel*, rather than expressing my heart's desire to be reconciled and forgiven of my sins.
2. "I'm sorry for ________________. Will you please forgive me?" This acknowledges what we have done and expresses our understanding that we have need of forgiveness from the one we have wronged or injured.

You've probably heard it said, or said it yourself: "I don't feel as though I can ever forgive him." Forgiveness is not, first of all, a feeling; it is a choice. The feeling will hopefully come later.

Forgiveness is given in obedience to the Word of God. It is not telling yourself the offense never happened; but, rather, it is realizing that the person has wronged you and that your part is to forgive the offense. If you choose anger or wrath and bitterness, you will hurt yourself, and your relationship will not be restored.

We all realize that the forgiving of an offense doesn't necessarily mean that you start wearing a smiley face as though nothing ever happened. Depending on the incident, it may take years, or even a lifetime, to get to the place where you will never think about it again. But when you forgive someone of a sin, it frees you to begin the healing process that will allow you to eventually forget the offense all together, or at least not to be hounded by the emotional turmoil you may feel at the moment.

## PRINCIPLE 21: DO *ALL* OF THE ABOVE

This last point of biblical communication is to simply start applying the above twenty principles. *Knowing* the truth is not the same as *practicing* the truth.

By way of review, the principles once again are:

1. Put off the old man.
2. Change your thinking process.
3. Put on the new man.
4. Put away lying.
5. Speak the truth.
6. Work out problems daily.
7. Guard against Satan.
8. Quit stealing.
9. Use discretion when communicating.
10. Build up rather than tear down.
11. Communicate while filled with the Spirit.
12. Put away bitterness.

13. Put away wrath.
14. Put away anger.
15. Put away clamor.
16. Put away evil speaking.
17. Put away malice.
18. Be kind to each other.
19. Be tenderhearted.
20. Forgive one another.
21. Do all of the above.

Be careful not to fall into the trap of thinking there are too many things to remember about communication to even begin practicing them. The adage, "Small strokes fell great oaks" fits well here.

Take another look at these points and ask God to point out a few you need to work on first. Review these twenty-one principles and begin practicing them in your family discussions today.

# PART 3

# CARE IN A LOVING MARRIAGE

# NINE
# Pursuing Discipline

Why are there so many divorces today even among churchgoers? Why are there so many disengaged family members? Why do so many families seem to be unraveling at the seams? Why do so many families lack true harmony and companionship? We have all seen families that seem to be nothing more than bodies living under the same roof with each one going their own way.

According to McKinley Irvin's, Family Law website:[10]

- 41 percent of first marriages end in divorce.
- 60 percent of second marriages end in divorce.
- 73 percent of third marriages end in divorce.

My point in sharing these statistics is not only to make you aware of them, but also to let you know that you have a much better chance at a successful marriage if you stick with the one you have! The same website informs us that, in America, there is one divorce approximately every thirty-six seconds. That's nearly 2,400 divorces per day, 16,800 divorces per week, and 876,000 divorces a year.

While various factors contribute to the high divorce rate, I believe a majority of broken marriages can be traced to a broken, undisciplined life of a spouse (or maybe of both spouses). Sloppy, undisciplined living can accurately describe today's modern family. This type of living shows itself in such ways as not resolving conflicts, being late for work, mishandling of finances, or neglecting daily time with the Lord in His Word and prayer.

Additionally, in marriage, it is often difficult for us to see or admit areas in need of *personal* growth. But, how easily we notice character flaws or areas that lack discipline in our spouse! We know every time our husband is late to work. Or, we keep record of each time our wives overspend at the mall. Because of our human nature, our focus can become on fixing our spouse, rather than working on our own areas of weakness.

J. Oswald Sanders in his classic book, *Spiritual Leadership*, describes discipline as an essential quality for successful living: "This quality is placed first, for without it the other gifts, however great, will never realize their highest possibilities. Only the disciplined person will rise to his highest powers."[11]

In this chapter, I encourage you to focus on areas of personal development and to seek to become a better person for your spouse, rather than focusing on your spouse's weaknesses and flaws. Perhaps ask the Lord to reveal to you any areas (not even mentioned in this short list) which you can seek to improve in order to be the best mate you can be.

The duty of disciplined living is incumbent upon *both* spouses and it is an essential key to a lasting marriage. It is very hard to enjoy a meaningful, deep relationship with your spouse without some type of personal discipline and some measure of personal orderly living.

## DISCIPLINED IN MY SPIRIT

Solomon, speaking of the desirability of self-discipline, said, "He that hath no rule over his own spirit is like a city that is broken down, and without walls" (Proverbs 25:28). The applicability of this verse to today's marriages is obvious. If husbands and wives do not control their own spirits and lives, then the family structure crumbles and becomes more vulnerable to the fiery darts of the evil one.

## DISCIPLINED IN MY ACTIONS

Our thoughts are often focused on our spouse and *his* need for improvement or *her* need to change. The first step to being disciplined is to address it personally—be brutally honest with yourself and examine each area of *your* life. Ask yourself, "Am I disciplined with my time on the computer, on social media, in sleeping, in attending church, reading my Bible and praying?" "Am I consistent with demonstrating love to my spouse, meeting needs, and fulfilling my roles in this marriage?" Once this examination is completed, you must then resolve to die to your wrong habits and to follow Jesus by walking in His Spirit.

Some may say, "But, self discipline is just not in my nature.

I'm naturally easygoing. I enjoy a relaxed, freewheeling lifestyle. Schedules bother me." While your personality may be more easygoing, God does not provide an alternative to disciplined living other than disobedience. God calls us to a life of discipline and to taking up our cross daily and following Him. Our primary concern should be, "Since discipline is required of me in following Jesus, how can I become more disciplined and, in so doing, honor God by being a loving spouse?"

A disciplined person practices the seven following principles. As you read through this list of practices, try not to think about your spouse. Instead, conduct a self-evaluation. Focus on becoming the right person who can positively contribute to your marriage relationship.

## ACQUIRE THE ABILITY TO SAY "NO"

We usually chide the parent who fails to say "no" to a rebellious child who is demanding his own way, and rightfully so. Yet, there are times we must learn to say no to ourselves... and mean it!

While saying no may seem a simple matter, it may also prove one of the hardest to master. Under many circumstances, it is the root cause of many spiritual defeats. Paul told the church at Galatia to "Walk in the Spirit, and ye shall not fulfil the lust of the flesh" (Galatians 5:16). That is, say "no" to the flesh, and say, "yes" to the Spirit!

The inability to say "no," divides many couples. Individual schedules, personal agendas, the desire to please or impress others—these areas and more hinder marital relationships.

Committed couples learn to say "no" to choices that will pull them away from each other emotionally.

**Say "no" to electronic distractions.** It is at times important to say "no" to others. Our time can easily be wasted or less valued by another's prolonged phone conversation, visit, or lack of self-discipline. With today's wireless technology, how many times have we stopped what we were doing to answer a text or email that popped up on our device? We need to have the ability to say "no" to the vibrations of our phones and continue with what we are doing. As one who has already lived my "three score and ten," I can personally say from experience that nine times out of ten, it can wait. Learn to schedule a time to look at messages, but don't be controlled by the sound of your electronics.

**Say "no" to frivolous activities and harmful relationships.** Say "no" to activities that cause your time to be used in ways that damage, rather than help, communication and closeness within your marriage. Each of us has a limited amount of time, and we need to make sure all of it is being used in the *best* way for our marriage, rather than in *good* ways.

I have seen husbands and wives choose friends who modeled ungodly lifestyles that eventually led to the demise of their own marriage. Instead, we should determine to follow Solomon's advice: "My son, if sinners entice thee, consent thou not" (Proverbs 1:10). Perhaps you need to say "no" to the office party, the group dinner, or the questionable opportunity that has the potential to weaken your marriage.

**Say "no" to Satan.** We sometimes forget there is a real

war (of the spirit and flesh) going on all around us. Satan has one goal—to destroy you, your family, and your church.

Sure, we must say "no" to the devil when we are tempted with alcohol, drugs, fornication, and the like. But, we must also say "no" when tempted to skip church or Bible reading. It may be that Satan provides me with a bed of ease so that I need not pursue lost souls for God's kingdom. It may be that Satan tempts me to *not* reconcile with a brother or sister because "it might just stir up more trouble or ill feelings." Or, as he does to so many, he may encourage us to justify not tithing, not giving to missions, not helping the poor, or a myriad of other things God expects of us.

Be on guard to the devil's advances. "Be sober, be vigilant; because your adversary the devil, as a roaring lion, walketh about, seeking whom he may devour" (1 Peter 5:8).

James said, "Submit yourselves therefore to God. Resist the devil, and he will flee from you" (James 4:7). There is nothing more heartbreaking than the sight of a fallen Christian. Your spiritual life and marital relationship will decline dramatically when you don't solicit—and depend on—God's help in saying "no."

## BE HABITUAL

In response to something I had just done, a friend once said, "Pastor Calvert, I knew you were going to do that. You are *so* predictable." Whatever it was I had just finished was a matter of habit—I was known for it.

We are all creatures of habit, both good ones and, unfortunately, bad ones. When it comes to having a loving marriage, we must stop certain habits and develop others (similar to the "put off/put on" principles found in Ephesians 4:22, 24).

The disciplined person must acquire the spiritual habits of daily Bible reading, daily prayer, regular church attendance, witnessing, serving God, loving others, walking in the Spirit, and denying self. Likewise, every Christian couple should seek to form the habits of having daily family devotions, expressing love and kindness, communicating biblically, exalting and serving the Lord, and unity of spirit.

Someone has said that it takes twenty-one days to turn an activity into a habit—either good *or* bad. Now might be a good time to reflect and make a list of ten habits that you'd like to begin or quit. Stop the bad habits of pride, lying, overeating, looking at wicked or ungodly material, taking the Lord's name in vain, being late, and blameshifting. And, incorporate good habits of Bible reading, Scripture memorization, prayer, kindness, demonstrations of love, and any other specific habits that would strengthen your personal life as well as bless your family.

## CONQUER YOUR BODY

The human body is one of God's most remarkable creations. When we consider the millions of miracles just culminating in the birth of one new baby, we are awed by God's power to design and create the human body. Paul admonished Christians regarding their bodies. He said, "What? know ye not that your body is the temple of the Holy Ghost which is in you, which ye have of God, and ye are not your own? For ye are bought with a price: therefore glorify God in your body, and in your spirit, which are God's" (1 Corinthians 6:19–20).

Our bodies, then—the temples of God—should be dedicated to the Lord's service. Our *feet* should carry us to "preach the gospel of peace, and bring glad tidings of good things" (Romans 10:15). God has given us *ears* so that we can have faith to believe, for "faith cometh by hearing, and hearing by the word of God" (Romans 10:17). The *eyes* enable us to behold the beauty of God's creation. The *hands* are given that we might serve others. The *mind* should be dedicated to thinking on those things that are true and honest and just and pure and lovely and of good report (Philippians 4:8).

As wonderful as the body is, it was never designed to dictate to us what we do with it. In other words, our mind and body should be dedicated to making right choices. God has given each individual the power of volition over his or her own body. First Corinthians 9:27 says, "But I keep under my body, and bring it into subjection: lest that by any means, when I have preached to others, I myself should be a castaway." I could lose my testimony, respect, and ministry for one bad decision regarding my body—and you could too.

Paul, who was one of the greatest servants of God to ever walk upon the face of the earth, gave the reason he couldn't trust his flesh: "For I know that in me (that is, in my flesh,) dwelleth no good thing: for to will is present with me: but how to perform that which is good I find not. For the good that I would I do not: but the evil which I would not, that I do" (Romans 7:18–19).

One of my favorite and most referred to passages in all of Scripture is found in Romans 6:11–14. Those of us who desire to live in victory over our flesh must meditate on this passage, reviewing it slowly and purposefully:

> Likewise reckon ye also yourselves to be dead indeed unto sin, but alive unto God through Jesus Christ our Lord. Let not sin therefore reign in your mortal body, that ye should obey it in the lusts thereof. Neither yield ye your members as instruments of unrighteousness unto sin: but yield yourselves unto God, as those that are alive from the dead, and your members as instruments of righteousness unto God. For sin shall not have dominion over you; for ye are not under the law, but under grace.

Our bodies and lives are to be dedicated to God's service. God calls us to present our bodies as a "living sacrifice" to Him (Romans 12:1). When the body wants to be lazy, deny it. When it wants to overeat, deny it. When it wants to call attention to itself, deny it. When it wants to dabble with unsavory things from the Internet, deny it. Our body should be made to do exactly as God wants. "But put ye on the Lord Jesus Christ, and make not provision for the flesh, to fulfill the lusts thereof" (Romans 13:14).

When you think about it, divorce, for the most part, is all about the body. Adultery and fornication are still right at the top of the list of reasons people break their marriage vows and end their marriages. The "lust of the flesh" (which we are warned about in Galatians 5:16 and 1 John 2:16) wars against the soul and looks for the right time to strike. So, every couple who desires a marriage that is characterized by a lifetime of being in love must resolve in their hearts to never cheat on their spouses.

We each ought to follow Job's example. He said, "I made a covenant with mine eyes" (Job 31:1). In Job's day, that was pretty much limited to people he came across in day-to-day life. In our day, we are presented with a host of additional temptations for our eyes—and we must guard against these as diligently as Job did in his day. The improper use of the Internet and social networking has ensnared many a man and woman. Don't be another statistic. Get help now if you are leaning that way and struggling in this area. Destroy any thing or any relationship that is improper.

Conquering the body is necessary for a disciple of Christ; for a disciple is *disciplined.* The following suggestions are included to aid in beginning the process of conquering your body:

**A few tips for conquering your body:**

1. Realize the war zone you are in and the enemy you face.
2. Choose to "die daily" (1 Corinthians 15:31).
3. If you really want to jump start victory in your body, consider fasting all day tomorrow. Ask God to take control of your body and fleshly appetites.
4. Consider a good exercise program. You will

not only reap physical benefits, but your mental outlook will improve as well. Consider biking, jogging, or walking as a daily routine. Over thirty-five years ago, I realized that I often had difficulty concentrating when praying on my knees. Either my mind would start to wander or I started to go back to sleep. When that would happen I would stand up and walk around. Then I just started going on a walk every morning, and I no longer had to worry about falling asleep. I increased the stride so that, as a side, I would get adequate exercise every morning, and I can walk anywhere, anytime. This exercise might also work for you.

5. Consider asking God to help in controlling your eating habits. Then, study about a balanced diet. Learn how to eat healthier. A balanced diet and exercise will bring new life to anyone.

## DEVELOP A PRAISE ATTITUDE

Jesus said, "I am come that they might have life, and that they might have it more abundantly" (John 10:10). Life is to be enjoyed, and the disciplined individual learns to get the most out of life by putting the most into it.

The psalmist said, "Let everything that hath breath praise the LORD. Praise ye the LORD" (Psalm 150:6). Christians have the privilege of magnifying and praising the Lord for all He has done for them. Those of us who have accepted Jesus

Christ as our Saviour must begin every day with praise to God in our hearts and on our lips for our salvation and for a new day. Think about it—every day we are given is truly a gift from God.

To put on joy, we have to put off negativism. There is enough negativity in this world without bringing it into our homes. In addition to the negative attitudes that are so easy to pick up on our own, we need to be especially wary of the media that might pull us into negativism. Ask the Holy Spirit to point out to you the effect these have on you, and decide to put off all those influences that hinder your walk with Him.

There is no need to have a down-in-the-mouth attitude. Christians should radiate a positive attitude at all times, giving thanks for everything (1 Thessalonians 5:18).

A story is told of two men, Sam and Bill, who went mountain climbing one weekend. They rose early in the morning and drove to the base of the mountain they were to climb. Once there they made camp, then began the ascent. For a long while, they followed the trails that were already marked, but as they neared the summit, the trails ended and they were compelled to forge a path to the mountain's peak. At last they made it. As they stood there at the mountaintop, surveying all that lay before them, a great silence fell over the two men. Finally, Sam spoke, "Isn't this beautiful, Bill? I never envisioned so magnificent a sight. The mountains and valleys and the sky above are certainly God's handiwork. I've never felt so close to God, have you? What do you think? I mean, what are your first impressions here on top of the mountain?"

Bill replied, "I was just thinking that this was the first time

I ever saw the back of a buzzard!" Negativism is a habit that needs to be conquered with praise.

Greediness and a materialistic spirit are sure ways to bring on discontentment and a negative attitude. The curse of contentment is comparison, so learn to rejoice in the blessings of others without coveting what they have. As the apostle Paul told young Timothy, "But godliness with contentment is great gain" (1 Timothy 6:6). Learn to be thankful for all that God has given you.

It takes genuine discipline to answer life's trials with a smile. We must be convinced that "all things work together for good to them that love God, to them who are the called according to his purpose" (Romans 8:28). No matter how dismal the situation may seem, remember God's purpose is perfect and He never makes a mistake. Our goal should be to turn trials into triumphs. Claim Philippians 4:4 as your verse: "Rejoice in the Lord alway: and again I say, Rejoice."

Every member of your home should exercise a praising, joyful attitude. Husbands, when coming home from work, be sure to leave your problems at work and demonstrate a joyful spirit. Wives, joyfully greet your husbands and children after a long day of work, school, and other activities. Home should always be thought of as a happy place where an attitude of praise is prevalent!

## ESTABLISH THE RIGHT PHILOSOPHY OF PERSONAL DISCIPLINE

While the world says the purpose of becoming disciplined is

so that you can become a stronger, prettier, or more talented you, the true purpose of discipline is twofold.

First, we should seek to become disciplined in order to be more Christ-like. Paul exhorted, "Exercise thyself rather unto godliness" (1 Timothy 4:7). We must constantly and earnestly strive to become godly. In Romans 8:29 Paul instructed that those God foreknew, "he also did predestinate to be conformed to the image of his Son." We need to let God finish His work in us—the work of conforming us to the image of Jesus Christ. Just as athletes must train vigorously and continuously for a sports event, so we must work hard to become more like Christ; we must exercise the Christian disciplines that will build us up in the faith.

The second reason for becoming disciplined is to serve other people better. Paul said, "For we preach not ourselves, but Christ Jesus the Lord; and ourselves your servants for Jesus' sake" (2 Corinthians 4:5). The more disciplined you are, the more you can invest in and bless others. While the world is concerned with how much they can receive *from* life, Christians are concerned with how much they can give *to* life. The Christian's walk is our living for Jesus Christ and others, including our spouses.

How does your philosophy of discipline show up in your marriage? Do you expect everything to just "fall into place" or to simply "work out"?

Discipline in marriage is not only disciplining yourself to do the right things, but it is disciplining yourself to know your spouse and meet their needs. If you are not naturally affectionate, you may think that your spouse doesn't need affection. If you are not a natural communicator, you may think your spouse is happy to sit quietly for hours. So, an unaffectionate spouse will need to exercise discipline to give and accept affection, and a quiet spouse will need to become disciplined in the area of communicating and listening in order to enjoy a rich relationship. A Christian marriage is about giving, not getting.

As you develop a godly philosophy of discipline, remember that discipline alone is insufficient. If discipline is not coupled with a relationship with Christ and the desire to become more like Him while serving others, it will never bring honor to God.

## FOCUS ON THE FINISH

Remember when people said at your wedding, "They are so in love!" Could that still be said of your marriage? If not, what happened? What happened to the flame that once burned brightly? How long ago did romance vanish from the marriage?

Many couples begin their marriage on a bright note, only to never finish it, or at best, to merely crawl across the finish line. If they do remain married, they often refuse to talk out their problems, instead compounding them by doing nothing.

Too many marriages today are composed of quitters—people who have thrown in the towel. Yet, God expects a person to finish the job He has called them to do. We don't usually think of investing in our marriages as a "job," but let's face it, if you have a good marital relationship today, it is because the relationship has been worked on by someone (or two) investing in the marriage! Mark it down—good marriages don't just "happen." They take discipline to finish well.

The Lord, speaking through His servant Joshua, gave a good principle that we can apply to our marriages, "Only be thou strong and very courageous, that thou mayest observe to do according to all the law, which Moses my servant commanded thee: turn not from it to the right hand or to the left, that thou mayest prosper whithersoever thou goest" (Joshua 1:7).

Anyone can quit when the going gets tough. The spark of a cross word can turn into a bonfire if left unattended. As hopeless as a marriage may seem—and you may feel hopeless to the very depths of your soul—there is hope in Jesus Christ. But don't expect to resolve things your way. Observe to do what He has instructed, for His is the only way that will bring joy to your soul and success to your marriage.

## GIVE YOURSELF GOALS

The reason most families are in turmoil today is that they never intended anything else or strove to be otherwise. They haven't set goals to bring them to a successful marriage and family. Good families don't just "happen." Particularly today, with so much adversarial influence coming in every direction and in every form, we need the Bible as our bedrock and the Holy Spirit as our guide more than ever!

Now, I'm not one of those "power of positive thinking" guys, but rather, I'm a "power of biblical thinking" kind of guy. We need to plan on using God's Word as our guide and then put feet to our plans.

Jesus taught goal-setting through the example of sharing His goals with us. His goal for His time on earth is stated in Luke 19:10: "For the Son of man is come to seek and to save that which was lost." He had a specific task that He set about to do. He said to His disciples, "My meat is to do the will of him that sent me, and to finish his work" (John 4:34). Just as Christ established goals, so ought we to purposefully establish godly goals for our lives.

**Set goals so that you can more completely yield to God.** The individual who has ordered his day will get more accomplished in less time and, hence, will have additional time in which to serve the Lord. Concurrently, the individual's goals should be subordinate to the family's goals, for the family without shared goals will soon become disjointed. (Too frequently, one or the other family member's individual pursuits takes precedence over the need for family unity. This situation should not be the case.)

**Set goals to maximize your potential**. What can you do to be the best spouse you can be? Perhaps you can make plans for a great vacation next year. Consider making goals for saving money, spending time with God, going on dates with your spouse, and generally enjoying time together. Ask yourself, "What can I do differently to encourage and edify my spouse?"

Goal setting gives you renewed energy and hope. The Bible says, "And whatsoever ye do, do it heartily, as to the Lord, and not unto men" (Colossians 3:23). So, be specific and have fun with whatever goals you set.

**Set goals in order to glorify God.** If I had to choose

only one verse from the entire Bible to aid the new Christian in establishing his life before God, it would unquestionably be 1 Corinthians 10:31: "Whether therefore ye eat, or drink, or whatsoever ye do, do all to the glory of God." The ultimate goal of every individual and every couple must be to bring glory to God. If we fail in reaching this goal, we have failed in life.

## ESTABLISH FAMILY GOALS

The home should be a place of enjoyment and shared fun. If these qualities are lacking, we not only fail our marriages and family, we also fail God. Husbands and wives should have shared goals for their homes. What is your family purpose and what can you do individually to contribute to accomplishing that purpose? I would recommend the following family goals.

**Salvation**—Your primary and paramount goal should be that all family members receive Christ as their Saviour and begin serving Him. The day my son was born, my wife and I dedicated him to God. It was our earnest prayer that God would save him at an early age, for nothing else in life was of greater importance to us. As the importunate friend of Luke 11:5–10 was persistent in his entreaty, so we prayed each day for four years for Troy's salvation. Soon after his fourth birthday, God answered our prayers. What a joyous day that was!

**Scheduled time with God**—Spending regular time with God as a family is one of the most important goals you can implement. Family devotions is an area that will easily fall by the wayside if a plan is not in place. Establish goals as to how often you will have them (ideally, every day), what time of day you will have them, and what your method will be. Family devotions need not be elaborate—just the family getting together, with the father leading the family in understanding and obeying the Word of God.

**Quality time together**—At least one evening every week should be designated as family night. This night should be reserved for family activities and memory making. These pastimes might include playing table games, eating at a favorite restaurant, riding bikes, talking, going sightseeing, or maybe just planning the family vacation. It doesn't have to be fancy or costly. Some of the best memories and enjoyable moments are free. Enjoy being together as a couple and as a family.

**Financial stewardship**—As a couple, strive to live within your means. The failure to handle household finances biblically is a frequent cause of marital problems. Matthew 6:33 is a key verse for each family: "But seek ye first the kingdom of God, and his righteousness; and all these things shall be added unto you." I think we all realize that the acquisition of "things" does not guarantee happiness or joy in life; rather we're instructed to seek God first, with the promise that when we do, God's provision for us will follow.

Husbands, it is our responsibility to work hard in order to provide for our wives and families. Lack of discipline in working, spending and managing God's resources will eventually result in being ill-prepared for later life in the golden years.

Together as a couple, teach your children by word and example to seek God first, trusting Him to add everything else He wants you to have.

**Home management**—A primary way for a wife to bless her husband is to manage her home with grace and consistency. Goals can help women run a household with effectiveness and provide specific ways in which the rest of the family can be involved.

## THE DESIRE ACCOMPLISHED

You may be thinking, "What does all this about personal discipline have to do with a loving marriage?" Well, any one of these points, when left undone, can be the catalyst for the decline or even the downfall of a marriage. And all of them together, if applied, will put you on your way to a very happy and wonderful home life. So now what?

First, review these seven alphabetical steps again. Then, make a commitment before God that, with His help and grace, you will seek to become the disciplined person He wants you to be.

1. Acquire the ability to say "no."
2. Be habitual.
3. Conquer your body.
4. Develop a praise attitude.
5. Establish the right philosophy of discipline.
6. Focus on the finish.
7. Give yourself goals.

Then, start now! Don't wait until tomorrow or next week or for the new house or job. Begin with the small faults you've detected in your own life and take the steps needed to grow in those areas.

Finally, remember that the end of the disciplined life is to bring honor and glory to Jesus Christ. Abandon all selfish motives and instead strive to exalt Him. We need the power of God to attain this end because being a disciplined disciple of God means depending upon Him for His help and guidance. With God's grace, you *can* be what God wants you to be.

TEN

# Preferring One Another

I remember visiting our two oldest grandchildren when they were only two and four years old. Being in an especially generous mood, I pulled out two one-dollar bills and handed one to Raquel, our oldest, and then started to hand the other one to Nate. As I was handing Nate his dollar, Raquel's four-year-old voice, full of emotion, said, "No Papa, don't give him the dollar. Nate's allergic to money!"

Without even one lesson on "how to be greedy and watch out for yourself," little Raquel had succeeded in doing both. (If you are wondering if I gave her the extra dollar, I did. I thought any four-year-old who could think that quickly deserved it! But I did give Nate his own dollar, as well.)

The prophet Isaiah, under the inspiration of God, made this parallel in Isaiah 53:6a: "All we like sheep have gone astray; we have turned everyone to his own way."

The picture painted here in Scripture is that we, as

wandering sheep, follow the dictates of our own hearts and desires. We do what comes naturally and think only of ourselves, rather than obeying our Shepherd or caring for others.

We know that man, by his very nature, is selfish. Being taught to consider one's self or to love one's self (as is widely taught in our day) is a redundant exercise, because we are innately selfish and are by nature motivated by self-interest. Of course, we easily discern narcissism in others, but we don't so easily detect that same self-absorption in ourselves.

Satan was the initiator of what has often been referred to as an "I" problem—his focus was totally on himself. According to the Word of God, it culminated in Satan's expulsion from Heaven. Isaiah 14:13–14 sums up his vain proclamation: "For thou hast said in *thine* heart, *I* will ascend into Heaven, *I* will exalt *my* throne above the stars of God: *I* will sit also upon the mount of the congregation, in the sides of the north: *I* will ascend above the heights of the clouds; *I* will be like the most High" (Isaiah 14:13–14, emphasis added).

The sin of selfishness is bound in the heart of a child and doesn't take any time to be revealed when children are at play. How many times have parents heard the words, "That's mine!" or "Give it back. I had it first!" And, when children pile into a car, they automatically struggle to determine who will sit in the front seat or by the windows. (Being one of six kids growing up, I understand this one by experience!)

But, this sin doesn't terminate while we are children. Couples in marital relationships often demonstrate this same selfishness when deciding where to go on vacation, what to do with free time, or how to spend a bonus—new golf clubs or a new living room couch? Although such a question should be easy to answer or work through, often lengthy and heated discussions take place instead. Selfishness is revealed in a myriad of areas: "his and her" bank accounts, values, and bedrooms. The sin of selfishness, when left unchecked and uncorrected, will divide a family.

In today's culture of self-emphasis, desiring to be a servant to others is like paddling upstream. This preoccupation with self does not end with self-help books. Many pulpits in America have degenerated into podiums for discourses in psychology.

But God's Word commands us to turn our hearts from self to the Lord. The Bible guides us to "Trust in the Lord with all thine heart; and lean not unto thine own understanding. In all thy ways acknowledge him, and he shall direct thy paths" (Proverbs 3:5–6).

As mentioned in the preceding chapters dealing with principles of biblical communication, the antidote for selfishness is the Christian virtue of living for others. Learning to live for others is at the heart of Christianity. When writing to the church at Corinth, the Apostle Paul cited Stephanas and his household as an example of living for others: "Ye know the house of Stephanas, that it is the firstfruits of Achaia, and that they have addicted themselves to the ministry of the saints" (1 Corinthians 16:15).

While the world is steeped in all kinds of addictions—drug, alcohol, food, TV and internet addictions—Christian couples should follow the example of Stephanas' household: addicting themselves to serving others, especially those within their own families. Practicing this principle of selflessness within the home strengthens your relationships and equips family members for greater usefulness outside the home.

If you desire a selfless spirit to prevail in your marriage, there are several biblical qualities you need to cultivate:

## LOVE ONE ANOTHER

Genuinely love your family (and friends—and, biblically, your enemies!). Fourteen times in the New Testament we read that Christians are to love one another. First John 4:7 says, "Beloved, let us love one another: for love is of God; and every one that loveth is born of God, and knoweth God."

Hollywood's definition of love emphasizes *feeling* good, but the Bible's definition emphasizes *doing* good. Love is demonstrated in a marriage when couples actively *do* things for each other and seek to bless one another. This love can be demonstrated in many ways—dates with your spouse, helping with household chores and "honey do's," gentle touches, and quality time.

Every marriage will have a unique set of ways in which spouses can demonstrate love. Find what works for your marriage, and do it. Surprise gift-giving is a demonstration of love that I particularly enjoy and that all of us could do more often.

When Mary and I had been married about ten years, as I was returning home from an appointment, I stopped at a shopping center. I immediately headed for the ladies' section of a nice department store and started looking for something I could buy Mary as a special surprise. I found her a nice skirt and blouse combination and proceeded to the checkout counter.

The young clerk asked if this was for my wife's birthday, to which I replied, "No." She then asked if it was an anniversary we were celebrating and again I said, "No." She stopped folding the clothes on the counter and asked, "Well, if you don't mind my asking, what's the occasion?"

I said, "No special occasion, I just wanted to get her something nice because I love her."

With her hands on her hips and a smile on her face, she asked, "Sir, do you happen to have a younger brother who is not married!" Every lady appreciates being remembered and appreciated—in whatever way it is expressed.

When it comes to loving one another, the important word to remember is *action*. Your love must be demonstrated. Make an effort to show your love to your spouse daily, not just on special occasions.

## SPEAK NOT EVIL ONE OF ANOTHER

Our self-love doesn't take long to flex its muscles when we feel that someone has hurt us verbally, either to our face or through gossip. Even in a close marital relationship, we can easily misunderstand or build a case against our spouse and then express our frustrations in a verbal rampage.

Modern psychology promotes vindictiveness and self-pity by encouraging individuals to "stand up for their rights." Yet, the Bible teaches that we must prefer our spouses by refraining from evil speech and judgment. James said it pointedly: "Speak not evil one of another, brethren. He that speaketh evil of his brother, and judgeth his brother, speaketh evil of the law, and judgeth the law: but if thou judge the law, thou art not a doer of the law, but a judge (James 4:11)."

It is not enough to refrain from evil speech. We must patiently work through differences and misunderstandings with honest, yet positive, encouraging words.

## PREFER ONE ANOTHER

Romans 12:10 clearly teaches God's way of living in relation to others: "in honour preferring one another." This requirement of Scripture may be extremely difficult in general life relationships, but it is also a struggle to accomplish in relationships with those closest to us, including our spouses.

Paul instructed in Philippians 2:3, "in lowliness of mind let each esteem other better than themselves." Preferring others and esteeming others better than oneself sounds like something for Bible characters—but for *us*? *Today*? What does that look like in my home and married life?

Well, for starters, and as difficult as it may be, instead of grabbing your favorite piece of chicken at dinner, offer the platter to your family before making your own choice. (Growing up with four sisters and a brother as I did, I might be thinking right now if I were you, "Yeah, if a chicken had four legs I could take a chance. But since it only has two, I'll take my leg first!") Instead of insisting on your favorite vacation spot, why not discuss the options with your wife? Instead of demanding help from your husband as soon as he walks in the door from work, give him time to unwind and switch gears mentally. Preferring one another starts with the little things. Every day, look for ways to prefer your spouse.

Selfishness is exactly what its name implies—living for self. It has no place in a godly marriage. Seek to bear one another's burdens (Galatians 6:2) and in honor, prefer your spouse at every opportunity.

## PRAY ONE FOR ANOTHER

No one is more deserving of your prayers than your family. Do you want God to bless your spouse? Ask him to! Do you want to love your husband more? Pray for him. Do you want God to change your wife's heart? Ask Him to work. Your spouse needs encouragement, strength, protection, and wisdom. Ask God to provide these things and trust Him to do it.

The common adage, "The family that prays together, stays together," holds great weight. Does your wife know you pray for her? Does your husband ever hear you praying for him? Do your children see Mom and Dad praying together for them? Praying faithfully with one another engenders family unity and weeds out selfishness. In 1 Samuel 12:23, Samuel told Saul, "Moreover as for me, God forbid that I should sin against the Lord in ceasing to pray for you: but I will teach you the good and the right way." Let that be the heart of your home relationships as well.

## LIVE FOR OTHERS

A selfless home is a touch of heaven, a refuge for hurting hearts, and a shelter in the time of storm. It is a safe place—a place where marriages are strengthened and where children first learn the true meaning of love. It is a place where family members can retreat and live in genuine acceptance. In a selfless home, both the husband and wife cultivate a loving environment, and the children grow to remember home as a place of love and security.

## OTHERS

Lord, help me live from day to day
In such a self-forgetful way,
That even when I kneel to pray,
My prayer shall be for others.
Help me in all the work I do
To ever be sincere and true,
And know that all I do for you,
Must needs be done for others.
Let self be crucified and slain,
And buried deep; and all in vain
May efforts be to rise again—
Unless to live for others.
And when my work on Earth is done,
And my new work in Heaven's begun,
May I forget the crown I've won,
While thinking still of others.
Others, Lord, yes others,
Let this my motto be.
Help me to live for others,
That I may live like Thee.

—Charles D. Meigs

ELEVEN

# Protecting Intimacy

When the bridegroom in Song of Solomon 7:6 exclaimed, "How fair and how pleasant art thou, O love, for delights!" I don't believe he was thinking that he finally had someone to do the laundry and wash the dishes. He certainly had other things on his mind.

As a Baptist preacher, I understand that most sermons on sex are denunciations of our society's excesses. Scripture warns against and condemns the actions of whoremongers, adulterers, and fornicators; and God has promised to judge them. While powerful preaching is needed to stem the tide of wickedness and promiscuity that threaten our relationships, I wonder if in our efforts to thwart the devil's lies, perhaps we swing the pendulum back too far to where the word *sex* is strictly taboo. As we teach biblical truths, I believe the beauty of proper sexual relations also must be accented, as sex within marriage is a gift from God.

Keep in mind that God was not only the one who invented sex, but He also wrote guidelines on how it is to be enjoyed. Scripturally, sexual relations are only encouraged and condoned within a biblical marriage between a man and a woman.

## A PRECIOUS GIFT

An important and encouraging study on this subject is found in Hebrews 13:4, "Marriage is honorable in all, and the bed undefiled: but whoremongers and adulterers God will judge."

A quick perusal of this verse conjures up the image of a bed with its four posts, mattress, and pillows. The word *bed,* however, is a translation of the Greek word *koita*, from which we get our English word *coitus,* meaning "sexual intercourse."[12] The Bible teaches, then, sexual intercourse is honorable, undefiled, and certainly not condemned within the parameters of a biblical, marital relationship.

Additionally, the word *honorable,* which is used to define marriage, is the Greek word *timios*, which means "held as of a great price, precious."[13] Marriage is a sacred union established by God, and physical intimacy within marriage is a precious, valuable gift. God views marriage as a priceless relationship.

## PREFERENTIAL LOVE

"Sexual dysfunction" is a euphemism covering a number of problems within a marriage. Generally, when couples experience problems in the bedroom, it's because of problems elsewhere in their relationship, such as a lack of communication, anger, selfishness, hatred, malice, money, depression, guilt, or other unresolved conflicts. Often, a simple solution for sexual dysfunction is to address and resolve these issues prior to sharing intimate time together.

Many times, selfishness (thinking too much about self and not enough about the spouse) is the root behind marital tension. As mentioned earlier, the antidote for selfishness, even in sexual love, is to prefer one another. Notice the encouragement given to the church at Corinth in 1 Corinthians 7:3–5:

> Let the husband render unto the wife due benevolence: and likewise also the wife unto the husband. The wife hath not power of her own body, but the husband: and likewise also the husband hath not power of his own body, but the wife. Defraud ye not one the other, except it be with consent for a time, that ye may give yourselves to fasting and prayer; and come together again, that Satan tempt you not for your incontinency.

## PURPOSEFUL DESIGN

In determining the proper, biblical role of sex, it is important to look to the first husband and wife and study the relationship they shared before the fall of man.

> And the LORD God caused a deep sleep to fall upon Adam, and he slept: and he took one of his ribs, and closed up the flesh instead thereof; and the rib, which the LORD God had taken from man, made he a woman, and brought her unto the man. And Adam said, This is now bone of my bones, and flesh of my flesh: she shall be called Woman, because she was taken out of Man. Therefore shall a man leave his

> father and his mother, and shall cleave unto his wife: and they shall be one flesh.—Genesis 2:21–24

From this passage, we find three attributes regarding the sexual relationship of a husband and wife.

**Relational**—Marital sex should be relational. A good physical relationship always begins with a good marital relationship, and a good relationship is founded on good communication within the marriage.

Some people believe that no matter what happens during the day, everything will be "all right" as soon as they cross the threshold of the bedroom. This, however, is rarely the case. Few people, women in particular, make good lovers after a long, frustrating day at work or in the home. Usually a harmonious sexual relationship is only obtained after there has been a demonstration of love, kindness, and tenderness toward your spouse throughout the day. If your wife's or husband's emotions have been frayed due to harsh or unkind words, gestures, or actions, and those problems have not been resolved, then there will be no enjoyment in the bedroom.

There will be times when your spouse may be uninterested in having physical relations when you are. When this happens, it is important to remember that proper sexual relations are not an entitlement at the end of a day. Rather, they are the culmination of a great and satisfying day with your spouse. They are the highest expression of your love and the giving of yourself to your spouse.

Both husband and wife should work continually at strengthening the relational aspect of their intimacy.

**Reproductive**—Sex was not only created for

companionship, but also for the purpose of reproduction. God's first command to Adam and Eve was to be fruitful and multiply: "So God created man in his own image, in the image of God created he him; male and female created he them. And God blessed them, and God said unto them, Be fruitful, and multiply, and replenish the earth, and subdue it" (Genesis 1:27–28).

Obviously, man is intended to reproduce. A privilege of the marriage bond is the child produced thereby. What a joy and privilege it is when God blesses a couple with children! (Of course, in His providence, God doesn't open the womb of some. While we don't always understand the reason, we seek to trust Him and His heart for us in these situations.)

Although God does not bless every home with children, it is natural for couples to want children, for this is God's ordained way of replenishing the earth. In fact, if a couple doesn't want children, they should probably examine their hearts to determine if the lack of desire is a result of selfishness. Is it that a spouse doesn't want to give up or change a career? Is it that a baby will interfere with their lifestyle? What *is* the reason? You may not want to have twenty-five children, but to not want *any* is an indication you should search your hearts as to why.

> Lo, children are an heritage of the Lord: and the fruit of the womb is his reward. As arrows are in the hand of a mighty man; so are children of the youth. Happy is the man that hath his quiver full of them.
> —Psalm 127:3–5

**Romantic**—Speaking of Adam and Eve, God said, "And they were both naked, the man and his wife, and were not ashamed" (Genesis 2:25). Adam and Eve possessed no shame or guilt in their physical relationship. Sex is to be the culmination of a romantic and harmonious relationship.

From the Song of Solomon, it's easy to see actions that describe a loving, romantic relationship—touching, stroking, and engaging. It specifically speaks of kissing, embracing, ravishing, desiring, and loving. We are fearfully and wonderfully made (Psalm 139:14), and God made our bodies to respond sexually as they do—it was His design. What is blessed of God should be sought with thanksgiving.

Romance in marriage is good and created by God. Don't feel guilty enjoying it. And, if this element of your relationship is lacking, take initiative to cultivate romance. For example, a couple's bedroom should be the nicest room in the house. It is wise to provide for music and candlelight. Attention given to these details will promote sweetness and a loving, romantic interlude together. There is no need for the "honey" to go out of a continuous honeymoon.

> Behold, thou are fair, my love; behold, thou are fair; thou hast doves' eyes...As the lily among thorns, so is my love among the daughters...Thou art beautiful, O my love....—Song of Solomon 1:15, 2:2, 6:4

## OPEN COMMUNICATION

Sometimes, it is a good idea just to sit down as a couple and talk about your love life. This is a topic many couples feel uncomfortable discussing, but if good communication takes place, the benefits are great to your relationship.

**Share your expectations.** Most marriages start off with an assumption that their spouse is going to be an amazing lover. Yet, in some cases, lovemaking is not as intuitive as it might seem. It is something that needs to be nurtured and worked on together.

**Share your desires.** Men and women bring different desires to the relationship. While most husbands are ready in a moment's notice, wives, on the other hand, need romance, tender touches, and thoughtful words.

Though it may be difficult at first, have an honest time of communication in which each seeks to ascertain how the other's needs can be better met.

## MAINTAINING LOVE

Song of Solomon 8:7 says, "Many waters cannot quench love, neither can the floods drown it." Many couples feel this way when they first "fall in love." But how can you keep this strength of love in your relationship over the years?

**Keep talking.** Many spouses suffer for years without sexual fulfillment in marriage. A common reason for this is the fear of hurting the other spouse's feelings. I can assure you, that more harm is done by this reticence than would ever be done by telling the truth. Eventually, a lack of honesty and openness can result in unwanted, negative feelings.

**Keep it private.** Further, every couple should do whatever is necessary to ensure privacy in their sexual relationship.

Children should be taught to respect their parents' bedroom, and should not enter it without an invitation. If you fear your children may forget to knock, it might be wise to invest in a lock for the door.

Additionally, be careful to not share intimate details about your relationship with other people. Special moments between you and your spouse should remain that way.

**Keep nurturing.** If you want to stay in love, commit to continually nurturing your relationship. You should plan a little getaway at least once a year. Not only does this provide a break from routine, but it also furnishes an opportunity for communicating love to your spouse in a completely private atmosphere. You don't have to go far, but make it special. Enjoy a nice meal out and plan an enjoyable evening together. You don't have to spend a fortune on this, but simply do what your wallet allows you to do.

## WHAT WILL THE CHILDREN THINK?

Your children's view of sex will be, largely, what they learn from you as their parents, both through teaching and observing your relationship. While parents are, of course, responsible to God for instructing their own children, often they are uncomfortable teaching their children about sex. But, if the parents neglect this responsibility, the children will learn by some other, usually harmful, means.

We live in a no-holds-barred era in descriptions, discussions, and graphics of sex. I recently read an article regarding a school textbook containing sexual innuendos that had been banned from Florida schools for the last five years. It was decided to put the book back on the reading list due to pressure regarding censorship.

While Christians may rightly get upset at the lack of discernment of public school boards, the sex education issue further underscores the need for strong Christian homes and alternatives to public school education. Parents alone should communicate the details of sex education to their children. Parents who are confused or uncomfortable about their own marital relations will likely bequeath uncertain values, faulty knowledge, and a poor attitude about sex to their children.

Not only do I want to nurture my own loving marriage, I want my children to have the same pursuit. The Bible, not our thoughts, is the final authority for life and godliness. Christian parents should teach that biblical sexual relations are a sacred part of a healthy marriage.

Consider the following tips as you seek to biblically instruct your children:

- **Answer every question your child raises regarding sex.**
  I heard a story of a mom who told her six-year-old son to go and tell his dad that dinner would be ready shortly. So the boy went out into the garage and found his dad and said, "Dad, what is sex?" The dad thought his son was awfully young to be asking, but he thought it was probably as good a time as any. So the dad tried explaining to his son about this uncomfortable subject in six-year-old terminology. "So, why did you want to know, son?" the dad asked after he had explained as best he knew how.

"Because Mom said dinner would be ready in a few secs," his son answered.

Never sidestep or disregard a genuine question from your child. Blessed is the parent whose children feel perfectly at ease asking about sex. If they don't hear it from you, they'll find their answers from someone else.

- **Explain the reproductive process.**
  It is my opinion that every child should have a fairly thorough understanding of the mechanics of this process by the time he is eleven or twelve. A complete explanation involving feelings and emotions should be reserved until just prior to marriage, unless asked sooner.

- **Teach your children about changes that take place in their bodies.**
  Parents should make sure they have properly prepared their children for the changes that will be taking place in their bodies at puberty. Don't let them find out the hard way. The fewer surprises, the better.

- **Teach your children specific principles of a Christian marriage.**
  Let your children know that when it comes to finding the right spouse, character lasts a lot longer than beauty. (Now if you can get both like I did—great!) Always emphasize character. Proverbs 31:30 says, "Favour is deceitful, and beauty is vain: but a woman that feareth the LORD, she shall be praised."
  Teach them that they are to marry "only in the Lord"

(1 Corinthians 7:39). In other words, they should only consider prospective spouses who have a relationship with God. I have advised single girls to date men who meet the qualifications of the man described by Paul in 1 Timothy 3 (whether or not he goes into the ministry). And I have counseled guys to consider marrying young ladies who strive to meet the qualifications of a Proverbs 31 woman.

- **Be involved in your child's social relationships.** Psalm 119:63 says, "I am a companion of all them that fear thee, and of them that keep thy precepts." Do your children's friends meet those requirements of fearing God and keeping His Word?
  Parents have the responsibility for guiding children in their selection of friends. Know who your child's friends are, and show a personal interest in them. Let your children know that they should not have secret relationships with anyone, and be doubly protective of your children using social media. Have strict guidelines for all of it.

- **Demonstrate a biblical attitude toward marital intimacy.**
  Children can pick up a worldly attitude regarding sex from the television, internet and worldly friends, either in the neighborhood or school—yes—even Christian schools. But, they will also learn a *biblical* perspective from just watching you, their parents. They will notice the way you speak to one another, the way you convey

respect toward your mate, the way you lovingly interact, and the way you enjoy the journey of marriage.

As we conclude this chapter on marital intimacy, let me encourage you to invest in the physical aspect of your relationship. Communicate freely with your spouse, and seek to honor the Lord and your spouse in every aspect of your relationship.

# PART 4

# CONDUCT IN A LOVING MARRIAGE

TWELVE

# Shew Thyself A Man

If you're honest, marriage is perhaps the least prepared-for relationship you've entered. While you've trained for your sports and for your job or hobby, very little training is given to men prior to taking on the role of husband. Other than watching our parents—and for some that wasn't so good—most know very little as far as a working understanding of the marriage relationship. Unfortunately, many of us expected that we would intuitively know how to be a good husband once we said, "I do." We subconsciously thought we'd receive wisdom that would enable us to perform well at our new post.

Being a good husband is truly a learning experience, and we should thank the Lord for wives who are very patient with us. But, if you want to stay in love with your spouse for a lifetime, you will need to take your role seriously.

King David, whom the Bible declares was a "man after God's own heart" (1 Samuel 13:14), had a son, Solomon, who was greatly endowed with wisdom. When King David was on his deathbed, he called his son to his side and charged him, "shew thyself a man" (1 Kings 2:2). With the drive today to become important, rich, popular, and successful, it is good that men remember this admonition. But, what kind of a man was David talking about? What kind of man does God want husbands to be for their wives?

Well, in the context of marriage, a husband can show himself a man by practicing loving leadership. In the paragraphs to follow, I've given a list of qualities that godly husbands will possess as they step up in leadership and "show themselves men" on behalf of their families.

## SHEW THYSELF A MAN OF LOVE

Most marriages stand or fall on the amount of love communicated by the husband. When I was a pastor, I had the joy of counseling hundreds of couples, and I can say that in most cases the husband's love (or the lack thereof) was a contributing factor to the success (or lack thereof) of the relationship.

The classic biblical passage of Scripture on marriage is found in Ephesians 5. In verse 25 the Bible says, "Husbands, love your wives, even as Christ also loved the church, and gave himself for it." We know that Jesus Christ died for the church because He loved us so much. His love was not based on our being good or righteous—because we were everything but! His love was based totally on His own goodness, grace, and mercy for us.

Likewise, your love for your wife should not be based on how sweet and loving she is to you—any non-Christian could love a perfect wife—but on your obedience to the Word of God in demonstrating Christ-like love. Jesus loved us when we showed Him no love at all.

Husbands have the honor, privilege, and, yes, even the command to love their wives. A man who biblically conveys love to his wife will have no problem at all leading his home. But if he is neglectful of this duty, his marriage will sicken. It will die without life-giving love running through its veins.

Most women *want* to be led by a loving husband who has her best interests in his heart. I have yet to counsel a couple where the husband was doling out sincerely loving leadership to his wife, and doting on her, only to have her reject his expressions of love.

We do not actually "fall in love"—we practice love. Love is giving of ourselves, expecting nothing in return. Love is mostly an action word. This means there are requirements for us as men, to *do* things for our wives. We can show ourselves a man of love through clearly defined actions. Here is my primer to start your list:

1. Tell your wife you love her.
2. Hold her hand.
3. Replace a burned-out light bulb.
4. Wash her car.
5. Be home in time for dinner.
6. Love the children.
7. Give her a sweet kiss.
8. Compliment the way she looks.

9. Thank her for a meal.
10. Praise the way she keeps house.
11. Keep the lawn mowed.
12. Paint the house.
13. Fix the furniture.
14. Replace the furnishings.
15. Send her a card on her birthday and anniversary.
16. Mail her an "I Love You" letter.
17. Take her out on a date.
18. Buy her a gift.
19. Open the door for her.
20. Help her put on her coat.
21. Be a good lover.
22. Provide leadership.
23. Demonstrate financial responsibility.
24. Faithfully serve the Lord.
25. Notice her new hairdo or dress.
26. Help in the kitchen.
27. Help to get the kids ready for church.
28. Have a good attitude.
29. Play games together and do fun things.
30. Understand her emotions and needs.
31. Be a good communicator.

32. Take a special interest in her house.
33. Brag about her good points to others.
34. Wrap your arms around her and embrace her.
35. Give her a night for herself while you watch the children.

Men, obviously, if we are going to love like Christ, we can never love our wives too much. Since the husband's goal is to love his wife as Christ loved the church, there will always be room for improvement.

Your relationship with your wife should be one that is rich and exhilarating. "Rejoice with the wife of thy youth" (Proverbs 5:18), and enjoy demonstrating your love to her.

## SHEW THYSELF A MAN OF LEADERSHIP

When the Lord was looking for a leader for "a great and mighty nation" (Genesis 18:18), God said of Abraham, "For I know him, that he will command his children and his household after him, and they shall keep the way of the Lord, to do justice and judgment; that the Lord may bring upon Abraham that which he hath spoken of him" (Genesis 18:19).

The work force is often divided into what is defined as "white-collar" and "blue-collar" workers. Being a white-collar worker implies one is in either a managerial or executive position. The blue-collar worker is the laborer or the one carrying out leadership's instructions. Within the family structure, the husband must wear both collars at the same time. He is both the executive (the decision maker) and the laborer (mowing the lawn, trimming the shrubs, painting the house, and helping with the children).

Since the "husband is the head of the wife" (Ephesians 5:23), he must provide leadership for her and your children. As the white-collar worker, you must seek God's will for your family and follow the Lord's direction. As the blue-collar worker, you must help carry out these instructions.

While leadership with love prepares the way for God's blessings in the home, leadership divorced from love is tyranny and is forbidden by the Scriptures.

**Leadership in Decision Making**—It is incumbent upon every leader to make decisions, and decision making is one of the first things husbands should implement. Although he is the one ultimately responsible before God for the direction of the home, this does not mean he sits down and decides what the family is to do and how to do it.

Though the husband has this responsibility, he by no means makes every decision. (All wives and mothers make plenty of decisions every day on their own!) However, poor leadership, or no leadership at all, from the husband sometimes pushes a wife into a role never intended for her. If the husband sits back and shirks his responsibility of being there for his wife and children, then the wife will often step up to the plate in order to make sure life moves forward for the family. The woman usually gets the blame for "trying to be the man of the home," but the truth of the matter is, the blame actually belongs to the husband for disobeying God and not providing loving leadership.

In making decisions, the man should always take into

consideration three things: the Word of God, his wife and children, and the circumstances. And, wise is the man who draws from the wisdom of his wife's counsel. "A prudent wife is from the Lord" (Proverbs 19:14).

**Leadership in Church Involvement**—As a husband, it is critical to lead your family in church involvement. The church you are members of should be fundamental in doctrine—one that teaches, preaches, and seeks to practice the Word of God. It should proclaim the gospel and should be a place where your children learn God's Word from an early age.

Since salvation requires "repentance toward God, and faith toward our Lord Jesus Christ" (Acts 20:21), we should find a church that preaches the whole counsel of God, one where the pastor is not afraid to speak out against sin and call for repentance. Your family must hear "how that Christ died for our sins according to the scriptures; And that he was buried, and that he rose again the third day according to the scriptures" (1 Corinthians 15:3–4).

Perhaps you know all this—that is, that you are a sinner, and that Christ died for you and shed His blood and was resurrected from the dead. Maybe you have always believed in God, the Bible, and Heaven and Hell. But it is also true that you could be like I was. I kept all that in my head and never experienced it in my heart. Salvation is a heart matter. (Romans 10:10 says, "For with the heart man believeth unto righteousness; and with the mouth confession is made unto salvation.") I was twenty-one years old when it finally sank into my heart that I needed to make Jesus Christ my own and receive Him as my personal Saviour.

I thank God for a faithful praying Christian mother and a godly girl, Mary, whom I had just met at church. (That girl has been my dear wife now for fifty years.) Most of all, I thank God for salvation itself—that the Lord convicted me that I needed to make a personal choice to receive Christ as my Saviour and that I did.

After I was saved, my participation in—and later my family's participation in—church became very important. I am thankful for the role church played in my life because of the huge, positive changes that took place as a result. And I encourage you to make church a central aspect of your family life, as well. Church should be the center of family activity.

Lead your wife and family to become involved in the work of the Lord, and help them exercise their spiritual gifts in the local church (Romans 12:6). Attend all of the services; be willing to teach or help in a Sunday school class; sing in the choir; give to missions; participate in outreach; and support the pastor. Help your children attend all the youth functions, and pray that God will make soulwinning and general church life an integral part of your family life.

**Leadership in Biblical Education**—God gave the responsibility for biblical education to the parents in Deuteronomy 6:4–9.

> Hear, O Israel: The Lord our God is one Lord: And thou shalt love the Lord thy God with all thine heart, and with all thy soul, and with all thy might. And these words, which I command thee this day, shall be in thine heart: And thou shalt teach them diligently unto thy children, and shalt talk of them when thou

> sittest in thine house, and when thou walkest by the way, and when thou liest down, and when thou risest up. And thou shalt bind them for a sign upon thine hand, and they shall be as frontlets between thine eyes. And thou shalt write them upon the posts of thy house, and on thy gates.

You and your wife have the God-given responsibility to teach and train your children for Jesus Christ. This responsibility is not something to be done merely on Sunday, but daily in the home.

Provide a regular time of teaching from the Word of God. Some call this the family altar, but whatever you call it, set aside a definite time of day for this instruction. Perhaps each family member can read a portion of Scripture, searching for the insights applicable to daily life. At the completion of the family Bible time, share the day's blessings, testimonies, and prayer requests. Close by encouraging family members to take turns praying, the husband concluding by thanking God for each member of his family.

Your wife will appreciate your leadership as a man of God in your home, and, while leading your family to love God benefits each member, it gives a special sense of security and peace to your wife, as well.

**Leadership in Finances**—Among the leading causes for divorce is disagreement over finances. And, though you as the husband may not spend every dollar or write every check, you are responsible for the financial condition of the home.

The subject of finances is an area where husband and wife need to be in complete agreement. With the exception of the surprise gift of a new grand piano I gave my wife one Christmas, we've never made a major financial decision without the other's consent and understanding. In fact, I don't think we have ever spent anything over $100 without the other's knowledge and agreement! What are some ways you can provide leadership in this area?

- **Decide on a budget and stick to it.** Often, an immediate impulse for newly-married couples is to indulge in a buying spree. It's important before a couple even says "I do" that they master the principle of being "content with such things as ye have" (Hebrews 13:5). That doesn't mean you have to settle for nothing, but go slowly. And then continue to remember and practice this principle throughout all your years of marriage.

- **Learn to live within your means.** The Bible teaches that contentment is a "great gain." Learning to live within our means is a principle that most of us have heard from childhood, yet it is so easily violated with credit cards. Adopt this principle: if you don't have the money, don't use the plastic. (If you find yourself under a financial debt load, seek counsel right away on how to budget your finances and pay down your debt.)

- **Honor the Lord with tithes and offerings.** One of the greatest financial principles for any couple to learn is found in Proverbs 3:9, "Honour the Lord with thy substance, and with the firstfruits of all thine increase." Make sure you never cheat God from the tithes due Him through your local church or withhold your offerings from God. As you seek to lead your wife and family in the area of finances, choose to be a generous giver. Ecclesiastes 5:13 says, "There is a sore evil which I have seen under the sun, namely, riches kept for the owners thereof to their hurt." Wise is the husband who takes this to heart—who understands that God gives to us so we can give to others—and then lovingly leads his family to further the cause of Christ through generous giving.

- **Don't judge based on indicators of wealth.** In providing loving leadership in the area of finances, it is important for us to realize that neither wealth nor poverty is an indicator of true spirituality. Although it is often inconvenient, it is not a sin to be poor. It's also not a sin to have wealth. How quick many Christians are to judge if they see someone they perceive to have more money or material things than they do. But the Bible says, "Every man also to whom God hath given riches and wealth, and hath given him power to eat thereof, and to take his portion, and to rejoice in his labour; this is the gift of God." (Ecclesiastes 5:19) Scriptures indicate that riches and wealth are a "gift of God," and who are we to deny someone their gift?

The man who provides loving leadership will, in most cases, have a contented wife who is thankful to follow her husband. Any woman desirous of pleasing God would love nothing better than to have a husband who she knew had her best interests at heart. But, regardless of how a wife looks, acts, or responds, it is still the husband's duty to provide loving leadership in the area of finances.

## SHEW THYSELF A MAN OF LONGEVITY

As you lead your wife and your children, be a man of faithfulness and commitment. Show your children a man who provides security and stability in their lives. Show your wife a man who loves God and loves his family. Show her a man who is committed to these principles for the long haul.

Show yourself a man—a man of character, a man of your word, a man of God.

## THIRTEEN

# Every Wise Woman Buildeth Her House

Right after God created Adam, He brought all the animals to him "to see what he would call them: and whatsoever Adam called every living creature, that was the name thereof. And Adam gave names to all cattle, and to the fowl of the air, and to every beast of the field; but for Adam there was not found an help meet for him" (Genesis 2:19–20). So after naming the elephants, alligators, giraffes, and everything else, Adam realized he had no one by his side like him.

So God caused him to go into a "deep sleep" (Genesis 2:21) and proceeded to take out one of Adam's ribs and then put him back together before he woke up. God took the rib and made a woman out of it. The Bible tells us that when God brought Eve to Adam, Adam was delighted: "And Adam said, This is now bone of my bones, and flesh of my flesh: she shall be called Woman, because she was taken out of Man" (Genesis 2:23).

The role a woman plays in marriage is serious business. If you want to be in love with your husband for a lifetime, it involves understanding your roles and responsibilities as a wife and committing to fulfilling them.

The Bible provides a perfect job description for the wife in Genesis 2:18. The Lord said, "It is not good that the man should be alone; I will make him an help meet for him." A wife is to be a "help meet," which means to be "a helping being,"[14] someone to come along side of and help. There should be no position more secure, more blessed, or more enjoyable than the woman's as she fulfills her biblical role of helping her husband.

Proverbs 14:1 tells us, "Every wise woman buildeth her house: but the foolish plucketh it down with her hands." This verse is not speaking of the physical structure of the house—the brick and mortar—it's speaking of the people of the house—the house as a home.

How can wives wisely and effectively build their homes? Scripture tells us of several key building materials:

## BUILD WITH SUBMISSION

A woman will never build her house as God intended unless she follows the principle, "Wives, submit yourselves unto your own husbands, as unto the Lord" (Ephesians 5:22). Biblical submission is not an inferior position, but it is, rather, an exalted position—one of honor. It is, for the wife, putting herself in a nourished and cherished position, as Ephesians 5:29 teaches: "For no man ever yet hated his own flesh; but nourisheth and cherisheth it, even as the Lord the church."

A wife's submission is not to be based on how loving the husband is or what he does for her, but instead submission is the result of obedience to the Word of God. Doubtless, it would be much easier to be submissive to the husband who is a loving, giving leader, but that is not the condition for submission.

The extent of the woman's submission to her husband is found in Ephesians 5:24 which says, "Therefore as the church is subject unto Christ, so let the wives be to their own husbands in every thing." Since the husband's authority is delegated from Heaven, he does have certain limitations. He is never to ask something of his wife that would be contrary to the Word of God or expressly forbidden by it. In like manner, the wife is under no obligation to do anything that would put her diametrically opposed to the Bible. In those cases Acts 5:29 would take precedence: "We ought to obey God rather than men."

## BUILD WITH COMMUNICATION

The wife who looks to the Bible for guidance and inspiration, and who applies the biblical precepts of communication found therein, is on her way toward achieving a home God can truly bless.

Satan wants to destroy your most valuable relationships: with your husband and your children. Fight his attacks by establishing your home on Christ, going to Him in prayer, and honoring Him in your heart and through the words you speak. Speak life, peace, and joy to your husband and children. Bless them with the gracious words you speak and the sweet spirit in which you speak them.

## BUILD WITH PURPOSE

Regardless of how many wedding anniversaries a couple has shared, a husband never tires of looking at his pretty wife. When your husband returns from a hard day's work, try not to be found in your old work clothes, kids tearing up the place, and a mop bucket in your hand. Instead, strive to look pleasing for him. A wise woman will try to eliminate as many distractions as possible (which is understandably difficult when several small children are underfoot) in order to provide a time of quiet communication with her husband. This kind of time may have to be planned far after the kids are in bed.

While you have several demands as a wife, mom, and manager of your home, do your best purposely to let your husband know he is important to you. What would make him feel loved? What would make him feel special? What is his favorite meal? Invest in and build your relationship on purpose, and God will bless your marriage for it!

## BUILD WITH JOY

The following writing from *Uncle Ben's Quote Book* causes me to believe that "Uncle Ben" knew the truth of following God's principles for a loving marriage and home. As you read it, consider how you might build your marriage relationship with joy, rather than with dread or frustration. How can you be a blessed, joyful wife?

## BLESSINGS FOR THE MARRIED

Blessed are the husband and wife who continue to be affectionate, considerate and loving after the wedding bells have ceased ringing.

Blessed are the husband and wife who are as polite and courteous to one another as they are to their friends.

Blessed are they who have a sense of humor, for this attribute will be a handy shock absorber.

Blessed are the married couples who abstain from alcoholic beverages.

Blessed are they who love their mates more than any other person in the world, and who joyfully fulfill their marriage vow of a lifetime of fidelity and mutual helpfulness to each other.

Blessed are they who remember to thank God for their food before they partake of it, and who set aside some time each day for the reading of the Bible and prayer.

Blessed are they who attain parenthood, for children are a heritage of the Lord.

Blessed are those mates who never speak loudly to each other and who make their home a place "where seldom is heard a discouraging word."

Blessed are the husband and wife who faithfully attend the worship service of the church.

Blessed are the husband and wife who humbly dedicate their lives and their home to Christ and practice the teachings of Christ in their home by being unselfish, loyal and loving.

—Uncle Ben

May we honor God and one another by having our homes established in Christ. May we each renew our commitments, so that our marriages will bring glory to God through our dedication to being *in love* for a lifetime.

> Who can find a virtuous woman? for her price is far above rubies.—Proverbs 31:10

> Her children arise up, and call her blessed; her husband also, and he praiseth her.—Proverbs 31:28

CONCLUSION

# When You Feel Out of Love with Your Spouse

So let's say you picked up this book with a marriage that is really struggling—perhaps even seeming hopeless. Maybe the very idea of being *in love* again seems out of reach. Maybe you feel so *out* of love that you don't even know where to begin. In these final pages, I'd like to tell you that there *is* hope—and guide you through some principles regarding what you can do right now.

Perhaps you've heard of the cynic who, in response to the guy that said, "Marriages are made in Heaven," retorted, "oh yeah? Well, so are thunder and lightning!" Remember this: when the sun breaks through the clouds after all the thunder and lightning, a beautiful rainbow often appears as a reminder of God's faithfulness to His promises.

"But," you say, "that's just not the real world because everyone has marital problems, and plenty of them." Sadly, that may be the way it is, but that's not the way it has to be.

If you and your spouse make a commitment never to let a problem remain unresolved, you can have a marriage that is more heavenly than stormy—a marriage full of rainbows testifying to the faithfulness of God.

God has not breached His promises concerning the blessings of marriage. His plan is not flawed. Then why are so many marriages failing? One counselor said, "There are basically only two things that cause unhappy marriages—men and women!" I suppose he meant that the only obstacles standing in the way of a wonderful marriage relationship are the two people involved. But the truth is you can change—with God's help. You can be *in love* with your spouse, even if the feelings you are experiencing now tell you otherwise. I want to show you how.

Let's look at one couple's marriage relationship to illustrate the importance of attitude. Michael and Sarah have been struggling through some contention that has strained the marriage. Sarah is ready to throw in the towel, but Michael, realizing his own shortcomings, has determined to be the blessing to his wife that he should have been all along. He sets out to do little things to show her that he loves her: flowers, notes, sweet words, acts of kindness, but nothing he can say or do changes her heart.

Why is that? The reason Sarah is untouched is the attitude she clings to. With a bitter heart, she says, "I dare you to be a blessing to me!" It is Sarah's wrong attitude that is at fault, not Michael's failure to offer affection.

The same thing could be true of you as you read. If your attitude is "I don't care what this says, my marriage is too far gone to be helped," you're probably right. If you have the attitude, "There is no point in trying. There's no love left to salvage," there probably never will be. If you come to this conclusion saying, "I dare you to teach me something that will change my feelings for my spouse," you probably will never change. If, however, you read this conclusion with the attitude, "I'd like to learn something, and I am willing to change," then God can do something that you never thought possible.

## UNDERSTAND THAT MARRIAGE IS WORK

In my thirty-five years of pastoring and counseling experience, it seems as though I have dealt with almost every type of problem a couple can have. Frankly, in my fifty years of marriage, Mary and I have had problems that we have had to work through as well.

In every marriage, problems arise between the husband and wife. For some, those problems are encountered almost daily. The truth is, however, that problems never destroy a marriage. Trying to live with *unresolved* problems is what destroys a marriage.

By following the principles set forth in the Word of God, you can resolve your problems. You can revel in a marriage that is free of turmoil and strife. Achieving this will be a battle, but God is well able to win the victory. You must, therefore, prepare yourself for warfare by learning Satan's tactics for destroying marriages. He has an arsenal of weapons to hurl at marriages, yet he has nothing new.

As we study the stiff-necked Israelites in the book of

Malachi and the many ways they offended God, we find what looks more like an editorial commentary on America today than something that took place 2,400 years ago. Satan is using the same strategies he has been using for thousands of years. Rather than repeat history, let's learn from the problems these people experienced and determine to leave no unresolved problems in our own marriages.

## THERE ARE NO NEW PROBLEMS

The old Testament prophet Malachi, whose name literally means "messenger," came to Judah (the southern tribe of Israel) with a message from God: "Judah hath dealt treacherously, and an abomination is committed in Israel and in Jerusalem; for Judah hath profaned the holiness of the Lord which he loved, and hath married the daughter of a strange god" (Malachi 2:11).

It seems that the inhabitants of Judah, having already spent years in captivity because of their wickedness, still had not learned their lessons.

They had defiled themselves by worshipping false deities; and, though God had warned His people over and over about their sin, and though He waited patiently for them to return to Him, they would not. Because of their unwillingness to repent, God allowed their conquest, and the people were taken into captivity by the Babylonians around 600 bc, with the final deportation at 586 bc.

During their Babylonian captivity, God orchestrated the fall of Babylon to Cyrus, king of Persia, and at His appointed time, God moved the heart of Cyrus to decree that the Jews be permitted to return to Jerusalem in Judah, at which time some of the people did return.

But during their seventy years of captivity, the land had not been left empty. Other people—heathens who worshipped false gods and practiced pagan religions—moved into the land, and now the Jews who had returned to the area from Babylon, influenced by these idolatrous people, were committing an abomination, something absolutely detestable and abhorrent to Almighty God, so much so that God sent Malachi to them with His message: *"Judah hath dealt treacherously, and an abomination is committed in Israel and in Jerusalem."* What was it that God found to be so offensive? Over the next several paragraphs, we'll uncover eight problems with the men in Judah and parallel those problems to our marriages. In order to stay *in love,* we have to know the problems that keep us from doing so.

## 1. A Disregard for God's Holiness

Your concept of God's holiness determines your attitude toward sin. When a man forgets that God is holy and that He abhors and judges sin, he is easily drawn into every kind of deplorable musing and action with no thought for how his sin heaps profound grief upon God or inevitable consequences upon himself or his marriage.

In Malachi 2, we find Judah in this condition. These people, chosen by God to be His very own, had lost their reverence and respect for Him. Their blatant disregard had manifested itself into actions God called treacherous and abominable, actions that profaned

His very holiness. They intermarried with pagans, "the daughter of a strange god."

God was adamant that the nation of Israel not be corrupted by the surrounding nations and their heathen idolatry because Israel was the nation and people through which He would send the Messiah to the world. God had specifically told the Jews that they were never to marry outside the Jewish nation, yet they blatantly violated God's restriction because they didn't care about God, His holiness, or His Word.

American culture has deteriorated to the point that we have assumed, even embraced, the same irreverent attitude toward God. We have lost our fear of God, and sadly, we see this lack of fear manifested in the obvious disregard that even professing Christians have for God's Word. The appalling divorce rate amongst Christians is only one example. But, really, our sin runs deeper than that. If we choose to look where God looks—our hearts—we will find what is at the root of it all: pride, bitterness, selfishness, and envy, to name just a few.

Though we do not see our sin as deplorable, God does. In verse 12, we see how God feels about the sins of His people, sins that hinder our human relationships and, worse, our relationship with God: "The LORD will cut off the man that doeth this, the master and the scholar…" The persons mentioned here are those who profaned the holiness of God in marrying ungodly heathens who did not believe in the God of Israel. God said He would cut off the man that did this. He further added that He would not receive their offering brought with tears.

We cannot expect that God will receive our offering of prayers if we choose to disrespect and profane the holiness of God in clinging to our pride and all the sin that it engenders. Obedience to God and His Word is imperative to having a blessed and happy marriage.

## 2. An Unrepentant Spirit

When a believer acts in a manner disrespectful toward God, when he commits any sin, the fellowship between that believer and God is broken. God tells His people in this passage that until they repent of their sin, He will not listen to their cries, nor will He accept their offerings of worship. "And this have ye done again, covering the altar of the LORD with tears, with weeping, and with crying out, insomuch that he regardeth not the offering any more, or receiveth it with good will at your hand" (Malachi 2:13). He is unimpressed by their show of tears. Repentance is what He requires of His erring people, and repentance is a huge step toward a loving relationship with your spouse.

## 3. Broken Vows

The Bible said that the men were not only marrying unbelieving women but also divorcing their own wives to do it. It seems that upon returning to Judah, many of these men became enamored with the heathen women that occupied the land, and their wives suddenly did not look so desirable.

I suppose their reasons for acting in this abominable way are the same reasons people have today. Whatever the process of thinking, this sin became widespread as people adopted the "everyone is doing it" mindset.

The people profaned the holiness of the Lord not only in disregarding His commandment concerning intermarriage but also in breaching the vows they had sworn before their God. These vows were a holy obligation.

Marriage is a covenant, a promise. It is a covenant made to your spouse, made before God. God witnesses the oath and joins them together as one flesh—for life. It is then that they are recognized as husband and wife. In God's eyes, they are as married at that moment as they will be after their honeymoon because marriage is not based on sex, but on the covenant. God said that in breaking this vow, the Israelites were dealing treacherously with their wives and committing an act that He hates.

God reminds them in the last half of the verse 14, "yet is she thy companion, and the wife of thy covenant." Once a man and a woman enter into a marriage covenant—a promise before God to be joined to the other person—that is the end of the matter. Your marriage is a covenant, a solemn promise entered into together, a promise to stay married to one another until death. That is God's plan for marriage—together for life. Marriage is about being true to your promise. Feelings of love may come or go, but the promise is permanent.

## 4. Pretentious Worship

The people decided they were going to do the things they wanted to do and live the way they wanted to live. Even so, they continued going to the temple as though nothing had changed. God said that those who were profaning His holiness by divorcing their wives and intermarrying with the heathen, He could not bless.

They responded with a question—as if God had not already spoken very plainly through His prophet—"Wherefore?" In one word they were asking, "But wait a minute, God. What wrong have we done? Look what we are doing to please you. We're coming here to the place of worship and offering up our offerings. What's more, we are coming with a flood of tears!"

Do you see the hypocrisy in what they were saying and doing? These men, after they had dumped their wives and married heathen women, went to the temple to offer their sacrifices at the altar and cry out to the very God whom they were disrespecting with their sin.

But God told them they had wearied Him. With blatant disregard for morality and righteousness, they disobeyed the one they claimed was their God. So, His ears were closed to their cries.

## 5. Erroneous Notions

For most couples, the first thing that drew them to their spouse was a physical chemistry—that tingle that zipped down their spine at the thought of their sweetheart, the light-headed, fuzziness and heart palpitations that caused them to swoon. Before long, their attraction grew into obsession. They couldn't bear to be apart. He couldn't get enough of her alluring eyes. She couldn't get enough of his disarming smile. If you asked either of the people if they thought their spouse was attractive way back when, the answer would be an enthusiastic, "Yes!"

But all too often I hear couples complain, "The feeling is gone." I am not denying that these feelings are powerful and exciting. The early days of romance are full of bliss. But our society promotes the idea that those strong feelings and physical attraction are what make the relationship meaningful. Americans have become so addicted to pleasure that they need another "fix" when that initial ecstasy begins to wane. After all, who wants to be stuck in a boring, ho-hum relationship?

When people say, "Well, I just don't feel like I love my spouse anymore." I address their grievance with a question: "What do feelings have to do with marriage?" They often look at me with confusion, but I'm serious! Certainly you would like to feel love as a part of your marital relationship, but feelings are never the reason for staying married. A marriage cannot be based on something as changeable as emotion.

Another remark that I have heard from discontented spouses is, "She is no longer attractive to me." The remedy for that complaint is simply to go stand in front of a mirror and look at yourself objectively. Try to see what your spouse is stuck with before you start condemning!

You may not be what you used to be, but physical chemistry ought to have nothing to do with the condition of your marriage. Wrinkles and pounds do creep in. Problems and responsibilities may douse the fire. But, the Bible doesn't say that we stay married only until we wrinkle and sag. It says until death do us part (1 Corinthians 7:39).

Actually, we have it good in America. In some countries

marriages are arranged. Because the parents are the ones making the arrangements, the bride and groom sometimes do not meet until they are standing at the wedding altar. I can only imagine what that would be like.

We had ample opportunity to scrutinize our spouses before marriage. We chose our spouses, and we made a vow to be faithful until death. Don't allow erroneous notions to change your commitment to your spouse. Feelings come and go. Don't trust them! Remain true to your vow, and cultivate love with the spouse God has given you.

### 6. An Unforgiving Spirit

In some marriage relationships, problems have been so severe or have remained unresolved for so long that, where there was affection, there is now loathing; where there was tenderness, there is now spite.

Feelings can swing from one end of the pendulum to the other. Such was the case of King David and his first wife, Michal. They had everything going for them. King David was enjoying great victory. Michal was married to a handsome, powerful king. They had everything money could buy. But their feelings for one another had diminished to the point that Michal absolutely despised David (2 Samuel 6:16; 1 Chronicles 15:29). What happened? What takes place in people's lives that they lose the love they once had for one another?

Like in David and Michal's relationship, many factors contribute to loss of marital love: incompatibilities, adversities, selfishness, even infidelity; but what happens more often is that people simply quit investing in the relationship the way they did at the beginning: He's too insensitive to realize that she still needs to hear sweet nothings whispered in her ear. She's too busy with kids and housework to sit down and watch a ball game with him.

Couples often say, "There's nothing there. We've grown apart. We just don't have anything in common." Statements like that are an admission that you are not contributing to the relationship. Keep in mind, it takes two to be married, and if you and your spouse have grown apart, you are at least partially at fault. *You* have responsibilities to your marriage. If there's "nothing there," you're saying, "I am putting nothing into my marriage."

I've got a simple little philosophy that you might find helpful: I'll get no more out of life than what I put into it. The same goes for marriage. What you put into it is what you'll get out of it.

When you persist in loving actions, loving feelings will follow. Feelings follow actions. It is a biblical principle that you love what you invest in. Matthew 6:21 says, "For where your treasure is, there will your heart be also."

## 7. Selfishness

In 1994, I read of a man named Firstenberg. From what I know, he was not a Christian man, and he wasn't necessarily speaking to Christian people when he made some studied observations about American culture. Nonetheless, I found some of his assertions to be noteworthy. He suggested that the 140-year pattern of continual growth in America's divorce rate—the highest in the world—is related to the "high cultural value" that Americans place on independence. He asserts that a culture that values independence encourages people to seek their own personal development rather than commitment to the family. It would be hard to argue that ours is not a culture that values independence over commitment to honoring one's covenants, especially the marital covenant. I have heard this statement myself from spouses who want out of their commitment: "Well, I feel trapped, and I want my independence."

I believe what the statistics really reflect is not so much a high value on independence as the magnitude to which selfishness has swelled in America as a dominating cultural malady. The stench of selfishness pervades a society when its people put their own interests above those of Almighty God.

It is clear that selfishness is the nemesis to healthy marriages. People often get married for selfish reasons in the first place. They imagine all that their partner will do to add to their own personal happiness, when in reality, they are committing to the other person's happiness when they take their vows. Marriage means that each partner in the relationship no longer has the freedom or luxury to think of himself first. Rather, each assumes responsibilities to the other as the couple commits to love and honor the other through sickness and health, poverty and wealth.

In your marriage, learn how to emulate the mind of Christ, preferring others above yourself. Serving others is the only way to find the happiness our selfish hearts desire anyway.

## 8. Marital Discontentment

John shuffles into the office unhappy about himself because of the way he had left things at home. Instead of resolving—right away, before going to bed, as the Bible teaches, or before leaving for work—the issue he and his wife Meg had argued over the night before, he left her upset, standing there in her bathrobe, struggling to get cranky kids ready for school on her own. Even the poor children seemed to be reacting to the tension that filled the air.

He sets down his briefcase with a heavy sigh and plops down into his chair just as Julie from the next office appears in the doorway.

"Bad morning, huh?" "Well, you know...."

Julie sits in the chair opposite John's desk and says, "I'm all ears."

As John relays the problems of that morning and the night before, he becomes aware of the soft scent of Julie's perfume. He can't help but notice how attractive she looks in the jade blouse she is wearing. "I never realized how green her eyes are," John thinks. She is quite a contrast to the disheveled wife he had left that morning.

Julie nods with a sympathetic smile. "I understand, John."

As she relates some of the same problems in her own marriage, John feels a little boost. It feels so good to know that someone else understands.

I'm sure you can imagine what ensued over the next few months as their meetings drew them closer together.

Unfortunately, this scenario is not uncommon. John and Julie are pretty typical. The initial excitement has faded in their marriages. At the same time, they are faced with pressures and responsibilities that take a toll on their relationships. They have two choices: stay and work on their existing marriages or take the "easy" way out and jump ship.

Is it any wonder that people jump ship, especially when the "lifesaver" looks so appealing? Think about our previous discussions regarding the ways our culture has influenced us: our addiction to pleasure, the prevalent me-first attitude, our irreverence toward God and His Word.

Along with those, I could add our discontentment and our desire for instant gratification. I've heard people say all too often, "I have found someone else." This someone else is usually more understanding, more attractive, more fun, more exciting to be with than the current spouse. Let me warn you as plainly as I can: thinking this way is a sinful and destructive thought pattern. This kind of thinking was prevalent among the Israelites in Micah 2, but God said: "Judah hath dealt treacherously, and an abomination is committed in Israel and in Jerusalem" (Malachi 2:11).

And as Christian couples, we should reject society's wicked influences and safeguard ourselves against illicit relationships. How can we do this?

First, married people should not tell their innermost feelings about their spouse to anyone besides their spouse, particularly someone of the opposite gender. Make it your rule to say only flattering remarks about your spouse to others. Griping and complaining to others is not the way to handle problems. If you need to talk to someone, go together to your pastor for counseling, and do what he tells you to do from the Word of God.

Next, safeguard yourself by avoiding situations where you are alone with someone of the opposite sex. Don't go out to lunch or to dinner with somebody of the opposite sex, for any reason, unless you have a crowd at your table. Obviously, it's fine to participate in office celebrations or meetings, but going alone with a person of the opposite sex is never proper. Do not make an opportunity for your affections to be turned away from your spouse and toward someone else.

You might say, "Wait a minute! That's just not the real world today. Everybody does it." And, I would say, "Not true." There are many of us that keep much separation from the opposite sex. It doesn't take much for the devil to confuse us when we are in a vulnerable position, even when we think, "I'll never do that."

We cannot afford to get cocky or arrogant about our ability to withstand temptations. I doubt that anyone stands at the marriage altar thinking, "I wonder how long this will last before I have an affair?" Most people don't think their marriage will end up as one of the statistics. The norm is that people enter into a marriage thinking that it will last forever. That's why they get married! Temptation to cheat always comes up later.

Finally, I implore you to guard your heart, "for out of it are the issues of life" (Proverbs 4:23b). Every affair happens after a process of wicked thinking. It may seem innocent at first, one spouse dwelling on the other's faults, but those first thoughts of discontentment are the seeds that bring forth a bumper crop of heartache later. Keep your thoughts in subjection to the Lord, and allow Him to renew your mind through His Word.

## SIX STEPS TO REKINDLE YOUR LOVE

If you feel you have fallen out of love with your spouse, I hope that the previous problems revealed potential reasons for your lack of loving connection. Having identified the problem is the first step toward restoration. We now know what to "put off." Additionally, the following six suggestions, if practiced carefully, will rekindle the feeling of affection you once had for your spouse. What can you do to actively rekindle that love?

### 1. Make sure of your personal relationship with God.

God made each of us with a spiritual vacuum, a God-shaped hole that only He can fill. The problem is that we try everything else to fill the void. People try to fill it with possessions, but things don't satisfy. Many try alcohol or drugs, but they are only a temporary escape. Religion is another source people look to for fulfillment, but only a genuine relationship with God can satisfy the longing you feel.

We must have a personal relationship with Him, but there is a huge chasm that separates us from God—our sin. The only way we can find our way to God is for someone to bridge that gap. That's what Jesus did when He stretched out His arms on an old rugged cross to die for our sins. He reached one hand to God and the other to us as He took the punishment for our sins so that we could be forgiven and reconciled to God. If you have never placed your faith in Jesus as your Saviour, you will continue to search in vain for satisfaction until you do. And sadly, you will miss the grace He wants to give you to help in all your other relationships.

No other relationship can ever be exactly what God intends it to be if you do not have a relationship with Him.

If you do have a relationship with God, are you going to Him for fulfillment and comfort? Or are you seeking other sources? Take the time to quietly, personally, and intentionally search your heart in this area. Do what it takes to draw nigh to God and then watch how your earthly relationships will begin to fall into place.

## 2. Consider God's perspective on divorce.

If you had a conversation with God about His opinion on divorce, it might go something like this:

"God, what do You think about divorce?"

"I hate it."

You continue, "Well, of course You do, but what about special cases? For example, what about the husband and wife who have tried to make it work for years but just can't seem to find common ground? They are always bickering and battling, even with children in the home. They are both fed up! What do you think about divorce then?"

"I hate it," God repeats.

"Lord, what do You think when the husband turns out to be a slouch, a couch potato, a complete jerk. Having put up with mistreatment all these years for the sake of the children, that man's wife would surely be justified in leaving once the kids are grown up and gone, right?"

God says, "I hate divorce."

"But God, when a wife has lost her sex appeal and doesn't

try to understand her husband's needs, don't You think divorce is the best option in that case?"

"I hate it," God says once again.

Do these words from God seem strong to you? Do they sound biblical? Well, look at Malachi 2:16 once again. The prophet says, *"For the* LORD, *the God of Israel, saith that he hateth putting away..."*

Unless there is the biblical ground of adultery, according to Matthew 19:9 and Matthew 5:32, then divorce simply is not an option, especially for someone who loves God.

This perspective can change your approach as you rekindle your marital love. Instead of looking for an excuse to leave the relationship, you can now look for ways to make it work.

### 3. Make a list of ways you have failed in your marriage.

Since you can do nothing to change your spouse, your own failures are a good place to begin. Analyzing your own actions and attitudes can be very telling. When you make your list, you may not see your failures as being the direct cause of your problems, but putting them on paper may be more revealing than you would have guessed. It may be that the problem is related to your spouse's reaction to your failure. Sometimes problems become more obvious when you simply take the time to analyze them.

What would happen if you started to examine your marriage to see where the problems may have started or how they were made worse by your own action or response? What would happen if your spouse made the same evaluation? If, at the very first sign of a problem in the marriage, you simply said, "Let me figure out how I have, perhaps, failed my marriage," and set out to work on those things, you might find out your home would be a better place to live, even for you.

### 4. Confess your failures to God and to your spouse.

When any relationship has been breached, the only way to reconcile the people involved is with honesty. Full disclosure is imperative to clear the air. You must tell your spouse honestly what you have done and ask for forgiveness. You must also be honest with your spouse about the pain he caused you, and then offer forgiveness. Once it is confessed, let it go. Forgiveness is the key to this whole scenario.

Confessing and forgiving within your marriage may take the help of a godly counselor. Do not hesitate to seek and ask for pastoral counseling. Be willing to take any step necessary to restore a loving relationship.

As you confess your personal shortcomings and failures, trust God to change you and your marriage. Notice, the key is to let *God* make the change. You can't change yourself, and it is certainly true that you can't change your spouse. You need the power of the Holy Spirit to help you to forgive graciously, to love generously, and to break old habits and thought patterns that have controlled you for years. This requires that both you and your spouse know Jesus Christ as your personal Saviour and that you fill yourselves with His Word. You will be amazed at the change He will make in you when you confess your sins and allow Him to do His work.

### 5. Set your focus in the right place.

When a spouse contemplates leaving a marriage, it is certain that he/she is thinking selfishly without regard for how divorce will impact the spouse or the children: "I can't stay with her," "I don't love him," or "I want to be with this other person." Notice all the *I*'s?

This selfish way of thinking is—plain and simple—pride. And God hates it. There is probably nothing He hates more.

Crushing your pride is very difficult to do because it involves changing stubborn thought patterns and attitudes. So, what is the remedy? I heard someone say, "Pride is not thinking less of yourself; it's not thinking of yourself at all." When your thoughts turn to what you want, what you're missing, how you've been mistreated, or how you deserve more, stop and ask God to forgive you for your pride and then redirect your thinking. Take your focus off yourself and put it on God first, then on your spouse, and finally, on your children. Turning the focus away from self makes selfish thoughts impossible.

Philippians 4:13 says, "I can do all things through Christ which strengtheneth me." Feelings have nothing to do with this. You can change your attitude, with God's help. You can do anything God wants you to do. And, with His help, it is certain that you can mend your marriage.

Put your focus, then, in the right place. Focus on doing your part, filling yourself with His Word and begging Him for help. When you do your part, God will do His, changing your heart. That's His department. Let Him do His job. Trust that He will.

### 6. Remember that marriage is a companionship.

God gave an important reminder to the men of Judah in Malachi 2:14. He said, "yet is she thy companion, and the wife of thy covenant."

Do you consider your wife to be your companion? What about your husband? Do you spend time together and enjoy doing life *together?* God blessed you with the gift of your spouse's companionship. Invest in that relationship and enjoy its blessings.

Plan activities for companionship. Make a list of things you can do together. Invite people to your home. Go shopping. Play games. Find something that you can enjoy doing together! But keep in mind, not every couple agrees on what is enjoyable. Figure out what it is you both enjoy doing, and do it together.

There are some activities you may want to avoid completely. In by-gone days, my wife used to love wallpapering the house. I tried to hang wallpaper with her one time in one of the bathrooms. That's the closest to divorce we've ever come! I'll never do it again. Ever! That activity was not a good companionship builder. I'm sure you have had similar situations in your marriage. Avoid activities that are sure to end in an argument!

Keep in mind that enjoying companionship does not have to be expensive. Maybe you could start taking walks or riding bikes. You can invest in activities that cost nothing—nothing, that is, but time. Time is the one investment you must make. You'll never develop companionship without investing time.

Take a few minutes and write down ten things you can do together. Ask your spouse to make a list as well, and then share the lists with each other. Choose a couple of the activities that are similar on both lists, and then do them together.

Remember, where you invest your time and treasure is where your heart will be. Invest in the most important human relationship God gave you, the one with your spouse. And, enjoy the beauty of loving companionship the way God intended.

## A FINAL THOUGHT

So, what are you going to do when you feel out of love with your spouse?

It's up to you.

You can either resort to your selfish and fleshly sin nature, or you can give yourself over to God and to your spouse.

You can continue trying to fix your marriage on your own, or you can let God work through you.

You can hold on to the hurt of old wounds, or you can choose to forgive the way Christ forgave you.

You can merely endure your marriage, or you can give yourself wholeheartedly to your spouse and start having a fantastic marriage, right now.

It is a wonderful feeling to be madly in love with your spouse. I highly recommend it! And, you can have that kind of relationship if you are willing to do your part and let God do His.

# NOTES

**Chapter One**

1. Jay Adams, *Lectures on Counseling* (Grand Rapids: Baker Book House, 1978), 250.

**Chapter Two**

2. Joseph Henry Thayer, *Thayer's Greek-English Lexicon of the New Testament* (Grand Rapids: Associated Publishers and Authors Inc., 1895), 42.

**Chapter Five**

3. Charles Hodge, *A Commentary on the Epistle to the Ephesians* (London: The Banner of Truth Trust, 1964), 270.

**Chapter Seven**

4. Zondervan Publishing House, *The Analytical Greek Lexicon* (Grand Rapids: Zondervan Publishing House, 1968), 197.
5. Kenneth S. Wuest, *Wuest's Word Studies From the Greek New Testament for the English Reader, vol. 1: Mark-Romans-Galatians-Ephesians and Colossians* (Grand Rapids: William B. Eerdmans Publish-

ing Company, 1966), p. 117.
6. W. E. Vine, *A Comprehensive Dictionary of the Original Greek Words with their Precise Meanings for English Readers* (McLean: MacDonald Publishing Company), 173.

**Chapter Eight**

7. James E. Smith, PhD, *The Ecclesia Epistles*, 2010, James E. Smith
8. Wuest, Kenneth Samuel, *Wuest's Word Studies from the Greek New Testament Volume I*, p. 117, copyright 1950, Wm. B. Eerdmans Publishing Company, 82.
9. Hodge, Charles, (2013), *A Commentary on the Epistle to the Ephesians*, London: Forgotten Books (Original work published 1856), 276-277.

**Chapter Nine**

10. (http://www.mckinleyirvin.com/Family-Law-Blog/2012/October/32-Shocking-Divorce-Statistics.aspx)
11. J. Oswald Sanders, *Spiritual Leadership* (Chicago: Moody Press, 1967), 44.

**Chapter Eleven**

12. The World Publishing Company, *Webster's New World Dictionary of the American Language* (Cleveland and New York: The World Publishing Company, 1960), 285.
13. Joseph Henry Thayer, *Thayer's Greek-English Lexicon of the New Testament* (Grand Rapids: Associated Publishers and Authors Inc., 1895), 624.

**Chapter Thirteen**

14. Carl Friedrich Keil and Franz Delitzsch, *Biblical Commentary on the Old Testament, Volume I*; (p. 86)